ONE DOG AND HER MAN

The Life of
Police Dog Bess

*To Jan for her support
throughout the years.
To Glyn
for his help.*

To Bess. Just for being Bess.

ONE DOG AND HER MAN

The Life of
Police Dog Bess

Ted Wright

MERESBOROUGH BOOKS
1992

Published by Meresborough Books, 17 Station Road, Rainham, Kent. ME8 7RS.

Meresborough Books is a specialist publisher of books about Kent with around one hundred books currently in print. These are listed at the back of this book.
  In addition Meresborough Books publish the monthly magazine 'Bygone Kent' which they launched in 1979. The cost in 1992/93 is £1.95 per month from your local bookshop or newsagent, or £21.00 (£26.00 overseas) for twelve issues direct from the publisher by post. A free sample copy will be sent on receipt of a 34p SAE.

Front cover picture by kind permission of Cecil Barton

ISBN 0948193 719

Printed by Headley Bros Ltd, Ashford

PREFACE

There will be one dog that stands out above all others in every dog handler's career. No matter how hard he tries, that animal cannot be replaced. All dogs have their own character but that one dog remains unique.

I became able to read Bess like a book, to recognise her every sign, to understand her body language. She in turn came to identify my moods, to be confident of my trust, and to know what was required of her.

The greatest compliment ever paid to me, however unwittingly, came from a Metropolitan Police Dog Section Inspector who was judging a police dog competition at R.A.F. Tangmere in Sussex. The weather was appalling with high winds and driving rain but Bess had worked her heart out for me. As I returned to where the judge was standing, he said, 'You and that bitch are a team.'

I could ask nothing more of Bess, who always tried her hardest for me. Naturally we were not successful on every occasion, but each time I knew that we could not have done more. While a lot of our duties were necessarily mundane, many examples of her work were outstanding.

Here, Bess tells her own story — with a little help from me.

Police dog training is based roughly upon the Trials Schedule. To help the reader to understand some of the expressions necessarily used, extracts of the Schedule are reproduced at the back of this book.

CHAPTER ONE

The Christening of Bess

My current police dog, Rajah, was coming to the end of his working life. Perhaps prematurely because, although he was a good dog in many respects in that he would track and search for me until he dropped, his temperament was becoming more and more suspect. He could no longer be trusted with strangers and was therefore completely unsuitable for any public relations exercises.

I was offered a pup with which to replace him and, to broaden my experience, I opted for a bitch which was to be donated to us by Bowesmoor Kennels at Bexley.

The water entered my nostrils and went into my ears. It went into my mouth causing me to cough and splutter. My coat became saturated and heavy. My paws, flailing frantically, grazed the side of the pond. Nails fully extended, I managed to get a tentative grip on the rough stonework and I dragged myself, still coughing, out of the ornamental pond.

A quick shake and the experience was fading. There were other puppies to chase. My two sisters and three brothers chased me and I chased them. We bumped into each other, rolling over and over in our efforts to gain the upper hand, then up again to pick on someone else.

Finally tiredness overcame us and, one by one, we settled down in the grass under the warm sun. One of the brothers, still a little playful, was lazily biting my ear.

I realised that we were not alone. There, with the Boss I knew, were two other men. I wandered over to them, sleepy but interested in the dark figures with the shiny buttons. I decided that I still had too much water in my fur so I had a good shake, so good was it that I almost fell over but not before I had soaked the two visitors' trousers as well.

It had begun a few minutes earlier when I first heard the voices. One I had heard before and, with the rest of the family, I got up and yapped excitedly. Even Mum, a lovely Alsatian, stood on her hind legs at the stable door and barked a welcome.

Over the top of the door came the weathered face of our breeder, blinking as his eyes became accustomed to the half-light of the kennel. Keeping Mum in there, he allowed us all to run out into the sunny day. It was great. We ran and we chased each other in the small paddock.

That was when I found that there was nothing under me except a few water lilies and some very startled goldfish. As I struggled to climb the slippery side of the pond one of the strangers came forward to extend a helping hand. I heard the Boss say, in his gruff Northern accent, 'No. Leave the bugger there. If she can't swim now, she never will.'

I did get out on my own but I wonder just how long he would have left me to struggle. After all, I was only seven weeks old. I am Bowesmoor Wynne. Born 17th June out of Defiant Rita of Bokra, by Bowesmoor Jarro.

A New Boss

A week after my first swim, we were all in the kennel again when I heard the voices. One was the Boss's and the other was just vaguely familiar to me. When the door opened this time, we were not just let out to play. Strong, safe hands lifted me gently over the lower part of the door and placed me on the dewy grass of the paddock. This time I felt curiously alone. Without the company of my brothers and sisters, whom I could still hear, the paddock seemed huge.

I wandered slowly and a little bit tentatively over to the pond. The lilies were still there and so too were the fish, which darted under them in a flash.

I realised that the two men were there again. One of them, a big man with a beard, was the man who had tried to help me when I went for my impromptu swim with the fish. I went towards him and as I approached I realised how big he was. I stopped and wagged my tail and hoped that they had not seen the involuntary puddle which rapidly soaked into the turf of the paddock.

The big man got down on his knees and took off the hat with its shiny badge. He did not look quite so big then. He said, 'Come on girl. It's all right. Let's have a good look at you.'

I tried to wag my tail faster than it is designed to wag and I found that my body wagged as much and seemed to overtake my tail. I got to him as quickly as I could, again hoping that the little puddle would disappear as quickly as the first. He rolled me over and tickled my tummy and I really enjoyed it as he talked to me all the time. Several times I heard him say 'Bess' but it did not mean much to me at that time.

Finally he stood up and I wandered around the paddock, feeling more confident now as I explored the places where I had played with my brothers and sisters and climbed all over my Mum. I had no idea that I had seen them for the last time and that I would never again run in that paddock.

I could feel the big man looking at me as he stood with his arms folded. I could hear words like, 'Nice bone. Good broad head. Likely to be long coated.'

The other stranger had gone into the office with the Boss. When they came out the big man picked me up and held me close to his chest. I did not like it at first and struggled to be put down, but he spoke to me all the time and I quickly got to like the feel of his strong arms and the warmth of his body. Different from the warmth of my brothers and sisters but nice all the same.

8

The pup settled in my arms as we walked towards the car park where our police van was parked. She was shaking slightly but nuzzled into my chest as I climbed into the front passenger seat.

I looked around and over his shoulder as he settled himself in the seat. Pausing only for a quick lick of his ear I looked at all the unknown pieces of equipment hanging up, at all the unusual things I later realised were the switches and loudspeakers that were to form part of my life from now on.

A Fresh Outlook

The van moved slowly out of the car park and down the drive. By lifting my head from where it nestled on the big man's chest I could see the kennels, where my brothers and sisters were, disappearing from view. Then it was out onto the road with houses and fast moving traffic, past green fields and trees. As we gathered speed all these things became a blur before my eyes. My tongue lolled out and I could not stop panting. My tummy felt strange and I could taste the breakfast I had eaten hours earlier. The big man spoke softly to me and opened his window a little. He turned me away so that I was not in a draught and I felt a little better. I turned my head to look out of the side window and what with the blur rushing past and the motion of the van, I again felt awful.

'We'll have to stop,' said the big man, but before a suitable place could be found, my breakfast felt like something that should not be there. Something that had to be got rid of. Although he held me away from him he was too late to avoid getting his trousers soiled. The other man laughed. I just felt rotten. The World still flashed by but I did not really notice. The big man spoke softly and stroked me gently. It seemed to help but I wished that they would stop for a while.

The van bumped off the road and onto the edge of a field not unlike the paddock where, a short time ago, I had played.

'Come on girl,' the big man said, 'Let's get some air and you'll soon feel better.'

He walked slowly ahead of me across the meadow, talking to me all the time. Many times I heard that word, 'Bess'. I did feel better in the cool breeze and I had to jump over the long grass in order to keep up with him. It seemed to amuse him and I exaggerated the leaps, and anyway, I liked doing it.

After a while he picked me up and we resumed our journey. This time I sat facing forward and, feeling better, found it quite interesting. Once, I forgot and again looked out of the side window but the feeling started up inside me again and I quickly decided not to do that any more.

The remainder of the journey was uneventful and I watched the scenery and felt the security of the man's arms around me. 'Wonder what my brothers and sisters are doing now?'

We turned into the steep driveway of the police house at Rochester, where I lived. Rajah squeaked in his compound as the van rolled to a halt. I got out, holding the little bundle of fluff very carefully.

Rajah

The big man spoke to the driver through the open window. The talk was of diet, feeding bowls and grooming gear, but all this meant nothing to me and, anyway, I rather needed to be put on the grass. The van restarted and I jumped at the sight of the puff of smoke from its rear end. I watched as the vehicle retreated down the driveway.

With a final wave to the driver, the big man carried me into the back garden which was about the same size as the paddock at the kennels. Are my brothers and sisters playing there now?

He placed me on the grass and, although he was still there, I felt alone. I really was quite sleepy but could not resist having a quick look round first. A sniff here, a quick dash there, all the time feeling the man's eyes upon me.

I suddenly became aware that I was standing beside a large wooden structure which was surrounded by the same wire stuff that had contained us back at the kennels.

Rajah

I had not seen him at first. He was standing quite still on the other side of the wire mesh. His ears were erect, his head slightly on one side. His tail began to move slowly from side to side. There was the biggest Alsatian I had ever seen.

'Good lad. Rajah, Steady,' said the big man, very softly.

The dog and I nosed each other through the wire, me more warily than him, I might add. I looked at the dark band above the brown eyes and at those immaculate pointed ears. Wonder when mine will be like that?

'Bess. Bess.' There's that word again. I looked round to see the big man crouching down and clapping his hands together. I ran towards him, almost falling over in my haste. He had a small bowl of milk. It was lovely. Not too much but very refreshing after my journey. I finished it off, moving the plastic bowl over the concrete in order to get the very last drop.

It was then that I noticed the lady standing in the doorway of the house.

The man walked out onto the grass. That word again. 'Bess. Bess.' It seemed to mean pleasure to me because when I ran to him he made a fuss of me and spoke in low tones. He walked slowly round the garden and I followed, stopping only to sniff things, and then having to run to catch up with him. Once I stopped to sniff something and a feeling came over me and I squatted and made a puddle. 'Good girl, Bess. Get empty.'

When I had finished, the big man was walking towards the house. I scampered after him as fast as I could. I came to two huge steps and no matter how hard I tried I could not get over this tremendous obstacle. I cried. I sat and cried. The man returned and picked me up. 'Come and meet her then.'

He placed me on the hard floor. It felt strange. I had never been inside a house before. It was fairly bright and with all sorts of smells. The floor was of a shiny material which made me very unsteady on my feet. Half crawling, half walking, with my nails fully extended to try to get a better grip, I made my way across the floor, following the big man as best I could. We went through a doorway and the floor became softer and easier for me to walk on.

I saw the lady in front of me, sitting on a chair. She was leaning forward to greet me. She, too, said, 'Bess,' in a very soft voice. I went forward but this time it was different. Something made me reluctant to go any further. The top of her face seemed to be covered in glass and I could see two puppies advancing on me. I stayed there, apprehensively peering back at them.

'Come on Bess. Good girl.' I stayed where I was.

The big man went and sat on the floor beside the lady's chair. 'Come on. Silly girl.' He laughed.

I went to him and to be with him, I had to be with her and very soon I had two people making a fuss of me. The lady stroked me and spoke lovingly. The two advancing puppies did not make much difference to me then. I got quite excited while I enjoyed the attention and hoped that neither of them saw the little puddle rapidly vanishing into the soft floor.

'Ted. She's lovely. Let's introduce her to Rajah.'

Ted, the big man, led the way and helped me down the huge steps. I was so tired but there was so much going on and lots to do. Both Ted and the lady walked towards the compound where that magnificent dog waited. He wagged his tail as he stood up. I went to the cage and he towered above me.

'Now. Steady, Lad,' said Ted, and opened the compound gate. The dog snaked round the gate before it had barely opened and he sniffed me all over and I do mean **ALL** over. I just laid down and this time I did not care who saw the puddle. Rajah then greeted Ted and the lady and went to explore his territory. I followed and occasionally tried to nip his back legs as I had done with my mum. Where was she now?

I was getting hungry by now. The journey had taken its toll on my breakfast and the drink of milk was all but forgotten. Rajah was given his meal. It was a huge bowl that I think I could have had another swim in. I went over to see what he had in it. He gave a low growl without raising his head, and I instinctively knew that I should go no closer. I had heard my mother make that noise when one of my brothers had become too keen whilst feeding from her and had scratched her with his needle-like claws. Believe me, we all took notice then.

Ted called me to him. I went to him to find that he had put a bowl of milk and cereal down. That was lovely and I only raised my head when the bowl was spotless and even then I moved it to one side to make sure that nothing had gone underneath it.

The big man wandered about on the grass with Rajah and me following. The milk and cereal soon had an effect on me and I did what nature had me do. Ted praised me. I do like that word, 'Bess'.

It was now late afternoon and I had slept for quite a long time on the carpet. Ted got up and once again, walked me around the garden. I obliged once again. 'Good girl. Get empty.'

Back indoors and he left me in a room with Jan and closed the door behind him. I went to it, not wanting to be left but all I could hear was the tinkling of a chain and Rajah getting excited, then all was quiet. I waited by the door for a few minutes and then went back to where Jan was sitting. I slept some more by her feet. My mind was full of thoughts of puppies and ponds, but I slept.

I do not know how long it was before I heard Ted come back and I was by the door before he had opened it. The door caught my foot but the pain subsided immediately as I welcomed him in the best way that I could.

I followed him as he left the room. Rajah was enjoying a refreshing drink after his walk. It was dark now and as we wandered around the garden, I could hear some strange noises and I must confess that this time, I stayed closer to Ted's heels than I had before. Eventually Ted, Rajah and I walked into the big compound, Ted closed the gate so that we were all shut in. Rajah knew what was required and, perhaps more quickly than usual in case I got the best place, was curled up in his bedding. It was very dark in the kennel but the smell of the big dog reassured me and, anyway, Ted was there.

He lifted me up and placed me into a box which was inside the kennel. The box was full of shredded paper which moved under my feet and was really quite snug. Ted stayed for a few minutes and then left, closing the compound gate gently behind him. I immediately clambered out of the box and followed him to the gate. He returned and gently but firmly, placed me back into the bed box. The paper felt warm and I lay down. Ted left the compound and as he went into the house I cried…and cried, and left the box. He returned and placed me back in the box but this time he put an old sweater of his in with me. This time when he left his scent remained for a long time and I snuggled down against it and watched as the house lights went out.

During the night I went along to see Rajah two or three times but I got very little response. I had a wander round the compound until I met a nosey hedge-hog as he came snuffling up to the wire in his quest for food. Rajah did not do anything so neither did I…except to get back in my bed and wish that it would go away.

Come first light I waited at the compound gate but no one came. I wanted to go out on the grass and in the end I just could not wait. I watched as the puddle transformed into rivulets and disappeared into the gulley at the side of the compound. Rajah came out of the kennel, stretched and looked with disdain at the puddle as he skirted round it to join me at the gate. He sat there so strong and erect, his eyes boring into the house. I got tired of just waiting so I played with his tail and paws. He lay down and sniffed me all over. I too, lay down beside that muscular body, feeling very secure. Wonder if my brothers and sisters are up yet?

I saw Ted moving in the house, and so did Rajah, for he stood up and wagged his tail as the man approached the compound. He had a lead and chain in his hand and he hung it on the compound gate as he opened it. Rajah jumped up to receive his fuss while I did the same but only managed to reach the man's knees. Rajah was then shut back in the compound, a thing that never happened from the look on his face. Ted walked me round the garden until eventually I found the right spot to do what I wanted to do. Ted was very pleased. 'Nearly a clean compound on the very first night. Good girl.'

Ted walked with Rajah on his lead, to the garden gate where he had quite a job to get out without me following. He managed of course, and all I could do was sit there and watch as they turned out of the drive and out of sight. I cried until I became aware of Jan standing behind me. 'You can't go out, Bessie. You haven't had your injections yet.' The words meant nothing to me but it was nice to hear the soothing tone of voice. She played with me until, once again, I had to go and find a place at the bottom of the garden. When I returned, she had gone into the house and I sat at the bottom of the steps and smelled the approaching milk and cereals.

I had finished eating and was playing with the empty bowl in the forlorn hope that it might, somehow, refill itself, when Ted returned. Rajah welcomed me briefly before going to check my bowl. 'No chance Mate, I've already done that several times.' He then went to the bowl of fresh water that Ted fetched for him and he drank noisily.

Ted sat on the steps and I sat beside him. He fussed me lazily as we both watched the big dog drink. Why did I get that sharp pain in my shoulder when Ted touched me there?

Later that day a man arrived with the same van that had picked me up from the kennels. Ted opened the door and Rajah jumped in. He then lifted me and placed me in the other cage. It was huge in there, but Rajah was only separated from me by wire mesh so I could see him and I did not feel afraid. When Ted got in the front I could see him too, although I was separated from him as well. The van moved off and I stood with my feet splayed as I swayed with the motion of it. I could see over Ted's shoulder at the hard road which was rushing towards us. I was just beginning to feel a bit queasy when the van stopped at the back of another house. I was carried out from the cage and into a garden which had a kennel in it, just like Rajah's. Ted put me on the ground and I soon began to feel better. He was talking to the other man. 'Short trips. Plenty of fresh air and she'll soon get used to travelling.'

The man's wife and two children came into the garden. I had never seen so many people in one place and I was a little frightened but only until the children got down on the grass and played with me. I liked that a lot but I wished that my shoulder did not hurt.

Later that day Ted came out dressed in his uniform. He took Rajah and together they went out in the van. All I could do was sit by the fence and wait until they came home. Jan came out and played with me several times and I know that she kept watching me through the window. She also fed me some minced beef and biscuits followed by some milk. Lovely.

During the next two weeks I went out in vehicles with Ted a lot. I was getting quite used to travelling and now enjoyed it a great deal. Rajah often went with

Ted when he was in his uniform and they were gone for such a long time that I felt they would never return. They always did though, and I would make sure that they had a smashing welcome and sometimes even managed to find them a present such as a stick or something.

I was getting quite fat and round now and my coat was beginning to shine a little even though I still had my puppy fur. Ted had only to appear in the garden with the grooming equipment and Rajah would go and stand with his feet up on an old tree stump that Ted used as a grooming block. He always finished off by giving me a little grooming session just to get me used to it. I enjoyed the bodily contact very much. 'Wonder when my coat will shine like Rajah's? Wonder when my ears will stand up like his? Wonder when my shoulder will stop hurting?'

One morning Ted put me into the cage next to Rajah's. It was nice leaning against the centre partition and feeling the dog's strong body beside me as I watched the world speed past.

This day we went somewhere I had not been before. Ted carried me from the van and into a building. A man in a blue coat was there to greet us. 'This the new one then, Ted? Sturdy little bitch.'

Ted placed me up on a table in a room that smelled strange but with a hint of other animals. Bottles and jars covered the walls. Pieces of shiny equipment lay on the work surfaces. 'Yes. This is Bess. Twelve weeks old and time for her first inoculation.'

He was a nice man whose fingers smelled of tobacco as he examined my mouth and looked at my teeth. He shone lights in my eyes, probed my ears and lifted my tail. I was quite pleased that he did it all in that order. He felt me all over, pressing my stomach. He put something cold against my chest and listened with his head on one side. 'Seems fine, Ted. Just hold her head.' Ted held me quite firmly and I felt secure even though I was perched up on a table. A sharp pain in my back leg but it was gone immediately. 'Next one in two weeks, Ted.'

As Ted put me back into the van my shoulder hurt me and I yelped as it took me by surprise. 'What's up, Bessie?' I wished I could speak but that pain went away quite quickly, too.

The next two weeks passed very quickly and were quite enjoyable as well.

Years before, I had obtained permission to go into Rochester Airport to do some training. Not many dogs are allowed in there and it was fairly safe for Bess to have a run with Rajah, even though she was not completely protected from infection.

I soon got tired though. I could not keep up with Rajah when he chased his stick. It was enjoyable but my shoulder did hurt after all that exercise.

After my next visit to the vet, Ted began taking me to work with Rajah. There were times when we would drive very fast and times when we sat still for long periods at a time on observations. The times I hated most were when Ted took Rajah out of the van at an incident, leaving me all alone in there for what seemed ages. Well, it is surprising just how large those vans are when you are just a

Rajah making his presence felt.

puppy! Sometimes there was a lot of shouting and I could hear Rajah barking, making his presence felt. Ted would put him back in the van and praise him while he did. 'Good Lad. There's a good boy.' I quite enjoyed hearing that, even though it was not directed at me.

One day we were driving along with another man sitting in the passenger seat. There was talk of stretching and squealing, of hip dysplasia and X-rays, none of which I understood but I somehow knew that they were talking about me.

Often, when I went to work with Rajah, Ted would leave him in the van and take me into the police station. I secretly liked the fact that Rajah was left behind. The police station was a huge place with many people and things to see. They always spoke to Ted and made a fuss of me and one lady always managed to find a biscuit for me, no matter what time we went there.

Another of my pleasures was when Ted put a plain coat over his uniform and walked me about the streets near the police station, where I saw lots of people as well as other dogs. I always wanted to give them closer inspection but was firmly but gently prevented from doing so. When Ted was happy that I was taking things in my stride we graduated to the High Street, among all the shoppers and their trolleys and prams. It was all great fun but those buses can be a bit big to a young pup!

The pain in my shoulder was getting worse. It still came and went but it was staying longer each time. I wished that I could have told Ted about it. I noticed it when I had been lying on a cold surface. When I got up it hurt and I sometimes could not help crying out. Stretching eased it a bit, but it only went away to return later. The trouble was that my other shoulder was starting to hurt, too.

Operational Set-back

I was four months old when Ted put me and Rajah into the van. He was not in uniform and I knew that today was different because Jan came out to see us off from the gateway. She also wished us good luck.

We drove a long way that day, further than I have ever travelled before, and I was glad when Ted stopped to allow us both to run in the woods.

Eventually we stopped in the driveway of a large house. Ted went in and was gone for some time. He came back and took me into the house. It smelled like the vet's I had been to before. He stood in the doorway of a large room and I looked in. It was all white tiles and shiny equipment.

This was the practice of a lady vet who specialised in hip dysplasia in dogs. After a detailed examination she declared that Bess's hips were fine but the trouble lay in the front legs. She had Non-Fusion of the Anconeal Process. The vet clarified it for me as elbow dysplasia and that it was present in both forelegs.

I left the surgery feeling very depressed. I knew that Bess was showing early signs of potential as a working dog but I had to convince my Force that it would be worth sanctioning such expense on an, as yet, untrained dog.

I left that telephone box in a different frame of mind. It had taken some doing and I must have caught my boss in a happy mood but he agreed to the operations going ahead.

We went back into the surgery. 'I've rung them and they've agreed,' he said as he lifted me up onto the table. Ted was obviously very pleased with himself. 'About what?' I wondered.

The lady clipped some hair from my foreleg. 'Could you raise the vein for me?' Ted did as he was asked and lifted my leg. The vein bulged as he applied pressure.

'That's fine,' she said as she inserted the needle. I did not feel anything really and watched as the fluid in the syringe became tinged with my blood before it vanished back into my leg.

I did not like what happened to me after that, but Ted was there and he had never let anything bad happen to me yet and his voice was comforting. I was suddenly very sleepy and I felt myself going over onto one side. A finger and thumb prised my jaws apart. I sighed.

The distant murmur of voices. The bright lights. The horrid taste in my mouth.

I lifted my head but had no control over it once it was up and lowered it as best I could, but still it hit the table with a thump. I opened my eyes.

Ted was standing beside the vet in front of a lighted screen. 'You see. The hips are fine but this is the piece of bone that I was worried about. I'm afraid that it is present in the other shoulder too.'

I was still very sleepy when a young lady in a white coat carried me into a different room and placed me in a cage. I had a scruffy little dog on one side and a cat on the other. I was too tired to bother about either of them really.

The following day, I went through much the same routine except that this time it was not Ted who held me and talked to me as the needle was inserted into my leg. It was not Ted who gently lowered me onto my side as the drug took effect, and it was not Ted's voice I heard just before I went to sleep.

Sometime later, I started to come round. I tried to stand but had no control over my legs. The pain in my shoulders was terrible and no matter how I tried, I could not get comfortable. What had happened to me? Where were Ted and Jan? Where were Rajah and my brothers and sisters? My thoughts were a jumble that I could not fathom.

When I next woke, I found the same young lady putting a bowl of water beside me. It was fresh and cool and served to get rid of the horrible taste in my mouth as well as being a reminder that I had not eaten for a long time. I lay on my side drinking, but spilling most of it so that it ran under my neck and into my fur.

I stayed in the cage for another two days. My legs were very swollen and I could see that a lot of hair had been shaved off. The rows of stitches stuck out like the hedgehog's prickles. I tried to bite them but it hurt so much that I bit the cage instead. On the third day, the young nurse lifted me from the cage and carried me into the garden. It was a bright, sunny day and I squinted in the unaccustomed light. The vet was out there already and I was placed on the grass in front of her. I stood there swaying for many minutes, afraid to move because of the pain. Even when I looked straight ahead, I could still see the rows of stitches out of the corner of my eye.

The vet and the nurse called and coaxed me. The girl crouched down and patted the grass in front of her. The stabbing pain as I made the first step towards her was terrible. I could not stifle a little cry. Coaxing words and soothing hands did little to make the pain go away and I was thankful to be picked up and carried back to my cage, which was now mysteriously clean and lined with fresh paper. I slept for a long time.

I was taken out later that day and on this occasion I was able to walk a few faltering steps. My legs were very swollen but the pain was constant, not the sharp stabbing pains I had had when I played with Rajah. I missed Ted. I missed Jan.

For many long days the routine was the same, but each time I was carried into the garden, I stayed there longer and was sometimes left alone. The sun was good and the presence of many animals meant plenty of exciting smells. I even met my first tortoise but he was not very exciting at all. There was still pain in my shoulders but the swelling was gradually going and I found that I could walk quite well.

Home and into Mischief

I had been put back into my cage after my exercise and was lazily watching the tail of the cat next door. Funny creatures, cats, so aggressive when you first meet them, but I do not really mind them though. I was contemplating whether I could reach that swinging tail when I heard the voices. I was not sure at first, but, yes, Ted was here! I was up and scratching at the cage door as he opened it and lifted me out. I licked him as hard as I could and squeaked with joy, the pain in my shoulders temporarily forgotten. As he walked me out of the building on my own lead, I saw that he had come in his estate car and Jan and Rajah were with him.

Oh. It was lovely and Ted had to get quite cross with me to stop me playing with Rajah so much. He, too, seemed pleased to see me.

After arranging a date for a check-up, we left the vet's for the long journey home. I soon settled with Rajah in the back and dozed as he examined my swollen legs. We were a family again.

For some weeks I could not go out with Ted and Rajah, and I was left in the garden when they went to work. I got bored and found that my shoulders were getting better as each day went by. So much better, in fact, that one day I felt able to dig a large hole in the lawn. I wished I had not, because when Ted came home he was not amused and I did not like that tone of voice one little bit. Rajah knew that all was not well as soon as he walked through the gate because he went straight into his kennel, reminded, perhaps, of a similar incident when he was a puppy. Ted also knew that I was getting bored so he was not too hard on me.

I did not dig any more holes, although on another day I did find a shrub which was not very well rooted in the ground. I was lazily chewing it to pieces when they came home. Ted was still annoyed even when I took him a piece of shrub as a present. No pleasing some people. Rajah went straight into his kennel. Ted took me by the loose fur around my neck and took me firmly over to the decimated shrub. He shook me and said, 'No No.'

I seemed to remember my mother shaking me like that a long time ago and I did not like that at all.

Later, Rajah and I crept into the doorway of the house and Rajah slowly wagged his tail. Ted looked up from his paper and I thought for a second that we were going to get told off again. 'Oh come on then.'

Both Rajah and I needed no second bidding and we, all three, had a mad five minutes until Jan sent us all outside before we wrecked the place. When I went out, I stayed well away from the remains of the shrub that caused so much trouble.

My check-up at the vet's in Surrey went well and I was now getting back to normal. My walks with Rajah became longer although Ted still restricted my rough play.

I was being extra cautious with Bess for two reasons. One was that the operations had never been carried out on a dog that was to work. The other was that it had taken a lot to convince my dog section to sanction the cost of the operations on an, as yet, untrained dog. I knew that she had the potential to become a good police dog and I had worked hard to convince them.

Now we had to prove it!

I overheard Ted on the telephone to one of his sergeants one day, and he was talking about my operations. Words like 'hereditary' and 'spaying' and 'retarded ear muscles' reached me but they meant nothing at all.

One day we were at Rochester Airport having a good game. Rajah and I had been running about for some time and on this occasion he stopped playing before I was ready to. I tried to get him to play some more by nipping his back legs and darting away. Instead of playing he put me in my place with a snarl and a snap which only just missed me. I do not think Ted saw that!

Blame it on the Butcher

I was in trouble again a few days after the incident with the shrub. We had all been out for a ride in the estate car, Rajah and I in the back as usual.

Jan decided to do a little bit of shopping before we got home. I parked and off we went, leaving the dogs to watch our progress as we left them.

Jan went to one shop and returned to the car to leave the purchases in it before we went on to the other shops.

I lay there for a while until the smell got too much for me. I just had to find out where it was coming from. Rajah just lay in the corner, not daring to move as I leaned over the rear of the back seat to investigate that delicious aroma. 'Ah. Yes. It's coming from halfway down in that shopping bag. Now, if I move this and push this bottle to one side.'

Ted and Jan returned to the car having finished their shopping. Ted surveyed the litter on the back seat and knew exactly what had happened. Rajah was just virtually cowering in the same place, knowing what was going to happen. How did he know, I wondered.

'She's eaten half a leg of lamb, Ted,' said Jan. Oh. So that's what it was. I had no idea, I only knew that it was tasty but the bones got stuck in my throat when I broke them up. In fact just then I coughed and a little piece of bone left my mouth and landed on the seat where Ted was leaning whilst he looked at the damage. I did a silly thing then. I leaned over the back of the seat to retrieve it. Well, don't want to waste anything, do we?

The back of Ted's hand crashed against the side of my head as he shouted at me. I did get one heck of a telling off, I can tell you. It was not my fault if the butcher had not wrapped it very well and they should have put a dog guard up to stop us climbing over.

I learned several lessons at the time but later I also discovered that lamb bones are not good for a dog!

Gently into Everything

My education was about to begin in earnest now and when Ted walked me, it was on a check chain instead of a leather collar. I did not like the chain at first as it was cold and it jangled. When I pulled it did not come with me. When I lagged behind, it pulled me and could not make up its mind what it was going to do.

It did not take long before I realised that, when I walked beside Ted and at his speed, the chain became unnoticeable and really was then more comfortable than the collar. When I walked in the right position, I got praise from Ted, both from his voice and also his left hand which would fuss my soft floppy ears. When will they stand up?

Ted took me to all manner of places, usually when he was off duty because then he had more time. Some of these places were pleasant, some a little frightening at first. One of the most puzzling places to me was the block of flats close to where we lived. The door opens with a rumble. We walk in. The door closes with the same noise. The floor moves under our feet. The door opens and we step out into a place which is exactly the same only it is different, if you see what I mean. It took me quite a long time to realise that when the floor moved we went up six floors to be spewed out into a landing which was exactly the same as the one we had left. Still, it was not so bad after the first few times and in the end I got into the lift before Ted did.

We visited bus depots where Ted obtained permission to walk me around inside the buses. They do not seem half as big inside as they do when you are on the footpath and they go rushing by. Some of the buses we went in had just been taken out of service and had a day's grime and rubbish on them. People complain about dogs but they should see what they leave behind themselves!

One place I found awe-inspiring was the railway station. Ted introduced me to it very gently. One morning we spent a long time in our local recreation ground which has a railway line alongside it. We stood on the far side of the rec until several trains had gone by. At first I was mesmerised by the huge things that made so much noise and seemed to go on for ever. By the end of the morning I was right up against the fence while the trains thundered by. They did not seem to mind me, so I did not mind them. Ted then walked me to the railway station and, after speaking to the Station Master, was allowed to take me onto the platform. A train had just left so there were not a lot of people around. Ted sat on one of the bench seats and I sat between his knees.

A man walked up to us and I presumed that he knew Ted. 'Just ceasing to be a puppy and turning into a young dog,' he said, and I thought that summed me up quite well. 'But what about the ears?' he added, and brought me back down to earth.

More and more people entered the station. Some passed by, some looked at me and made noises as if I was a baby in a pram. Two lads in leather jackets with what looked like check chains on them came noisily onto the platform. They made sounds like a cat at me as they stomped along, making other people move. Ted just smiled to himself. I guess he was thinking of the future. A voice boomed out above my head making me start. 'Steady Bess. There's a good girl.' Ted spoke softly, his hands had a calming effect on me.

'The next train will be to Gillingham, Chatham, Rochester etc. etc.' I just sat there, looking up at the loudspeaker with my head cocked on one side. People around us were amused and chuckled at me.

I heard the rumble and those same people began to stir. The train came in very fast and began to lose speed. The people moved towards it. There was a lot of door banging and a whistle and then I could see the whole train as it began to move, slowly gathering speed. I watched as the end of it fairly flashed past and out of view. Then there was silence and I looked up at Ted. 'There. That wasn't so bad. Was it?'

We stayed on the station until three more trains had entered and left and each time it was much the same. In the end I was waiting for the booming voice from the loudspeaker. 'The next train will be…'

We went to the Station Master's office and Ted thanked him for his help. That exercise had taken the best part of the day but Ted thought it was time well spent. He called it 'character building'.

Ragtime

Curtains For Me

Another 'game' that Ted used to play with me was to encourage me to pull on a piece of rag or a sack. I had a lovely time trying to get it away from him. My feet would brace in my efforts to pull him over, but I never could. He used to encourage Rajah to join in and pull on the rag with me and the dog always obliged, as though he remembered doing it when he was a pup. This exercise was to prepare me for doing manwork but it backfired on Ted and also got me into trouble again, too.

One morning I had been left in the garden when Ted had gone to work with Rajah. I was just wandering around, minding my own business. I found myself beneath a large round thing with 'rags' hanging on it. I did not pay much attention to it until a gust of wind caught it and it spun round causing one of the longer 'rags' to cuff me round the ear. I grabbed hold of the long stripy thing and pulled hard on it until it gave up and came down to join me on the grass. The stripy thing did not do much when it was on the ground but some white things were wafted across my back. I spun round and bit into those things that insisted on attacking me from above. I pulled hard and there was a series of clicks from up on the round thing and small brightly coloured hard objects rained down around me.

When I got home I was greeted by Bess as usual. Across the garden, under the rotary clothes line, I saw my pyjama trousers and a pair of net curtains which had been absoloutely ripped to shreds.

Rajah, being more shrewd than I, went straight to his kennel, leaving me to face the music.

Starting in Earnest

Most days when Ted was off duty, we would spend twenty minutes or so in a field close to our home. I got to know that whenever we went to that particular location, it was to work. Eventually, I began to get excited each time we went in that direction.

On my earlier walks with Ted, it had not mattered if I had walked a bit in front of him or a bit behind, as long as I walked on his left. Now I had to walk with my right shoulder against his left knee. The check chain would ensure that I did not get out of position because when I did there would be a sharp tug on it accompanied by the word 'Heel'. It was not as bad as it sounds really, because Ted's left hand was always there to praise and fondle my soft ears whenever I did get into the correct position. He always let me know by his tone of voice anyway.

As time went on we did right turns, left turns. We stopped suddenly and I had to sit immediately by his side. We did it at the run. We did it very slowly. All the time, I had to remain by his left knee.

It was all an exercise in control but at the same time built up the bond and necessary trust between us.

I loved the bodily contact and after each short training session we would explode into play, during which Ted would ensure that, at some time, he got down to my level.

As we progressed, I realised that the check chain was not as bad as it seemed. If I walked in the right position, I barely noticed it. It became an integral part of our games too, because when Ted had finished work, he would take the chain from around my neck and bait me with it before sending it spinning through the air. I would chase it, not daring to let it out of my sight. I would pounce on it and carry it back to Ted with just the slightest bit dangling from the corner of my mouth. 'Come on. Throw it again.'

I could take you to certain trees in Kent where, if you looked hard enough, you could see a chain hanging from the higher branches. The fruit of a bad shot.

I had always like to chase things and Ted would often throw things for me in the back garden at home. A ball. An old soft toy. A slipper or a stick. In the beginning, I would sometimes take them behind the kennel to chew them before Ted came to get me. Later, when he was sure that I would go and pick things up, he would coax me to bring them right back to him, and introduced more words, 'Fetch, Bess'.

When we went to our training field he threw a dumbbell for me to retrieve and this time he really insisted that I should take it right back to him. This was not a toy. It was balanced to rest across my lower jaw so that we could perfect the exercise.

Always we would finish with the silvery chain flashing through the air. I liked that a lot but I did not realise that even this was teaching me to pick up metal objects. Crafty!

Tracking Start

After a few weeks of this training-cum-play, I was able to sit and stay while Ted walked round the field on his own. The temptation to run after him was great and sometimes I succumbed to it, but I was always put back in exactly the same spot, quite firmly, and I knew that I had done wrong. I knew that he would always come back but sometimes it really seemed an age.

'Come on girl,' he said, as he opened the back of the van and I put my head through the waiting check chain. We were on the edge of a field I had never seen before. It was covered with lush clover which smelled sweet and fresh.

Ted made me sit and stay while he got something out of the van. It was a bright and shiny tracking harness. 'New one for a new girl,' he said.

He put the harness on me and adjusted many buckles. I did not like it very much and I shook, hoping that it would fall off. Ted watched me, then adjusted some of the buckles again. I shook again and this time I did not feel so cluttered up. I still did not like the smell of the brand new oily leather.

Ted put my lead and chain back on me and what with those and the new harness, I felt like a trussed-up chicken. He tied me to a post and I sat there feeling very forlorn and lost.

'What next, I wonder? Wait a minute. What's that he's got there? It's my ball. My favourite red ball.'

He tossed it up and down in front of me. I jumped in unison with it but it was just out of reach. I barked. I cried. I pleaded with him to let me have it.

'Look Bess. Look what I've got.' 'I can see what you've got but I can't do much about it, now can I? Now what's he doing? Oh. No. He's taking my ball away.'

Ted walked in a straight line away from me but every so often he turned and threw my ball up into the air. 'What's this then, Bess?'

He stopped about one hundred yards away from me and with a last flourish of the ball he placed it on the ground between his feet. Taking great care to retrace his steps exactly, he ran back to me.

I was torn between welcoming him and racing across the field for my ball. I was still tied so I checked his hands just in case, by some miracle, he still had my ball with him. No chance.

He untied my lead from the fence post and walked me to the edge of the field. I could not get out there quick enough. Who knows what could happen to a ball left all alone in a field? He held the lead right at its very end. 'Track, Bess. Where is it?'

I ran as fast as I could, pulling him along the line he had made in the dew. I could see where he had walked and his scent was strong. I ran and I pulled. Ted encouraged me.

'There it is.' Right in the middle of the flattened grass, where Ted had stood, was my shiny red ball. I pounced on it and mouthed it while Ted took off my check chain. I thought that he was going to explode in his praise for me. His

Tracking

voice was raised high and he leapt about with his arms waving. Anyone looking on must have thought he was mad, but he certainly let me know that he was very pleased with me.

After we had settled down again, we went through the same routine three more times. Each time we moved further along the field so that a fresh patch of clover was used each time.

I liked this tracking and got almost as much pleasure from doing it as from the praise at the end. On the last track I even accepted that I had to be tied to the fence when he walked off with my ball. This time it was buried deep in the clover and I had to find it by using my nose only, not my eyes.

We were having our last game. My harness was off. I turned to see a man standing on the edge of the field. Ted greeted the land owner who had his handsome black Labrador with him.

We had a good time examining each other and then had a run round together while the two men talked. As we went back to them, I heard the man say, 'What about the ears then? Will they ever come up?'

Ted explained about the operations on my shoulders and the fact that I had retarded ear muscles because of them. 'Still, gives her character and she'll certainly stand out in a crowd,' the man chuckled. He walked with us to our van and we all said our farewells. I liked that Lab.

The following day we went to the same field and I half expected to see the man and his dog again, but they were not there.

This time, when Ted put the harness on me, he attached a length of white rope to it. The rope had a clasp at one end which went onto a ring on the back of the harness.

When I went to charge off to find my ball at the end of the track, there was more restraint on me as, with nose to the ground, I followed Ted's scent to my beloved ball.

The harness came off and the ball went bouncing across the grass. I had been introduced to the most important aspect of my working life...Tracking.

A Change in Rajah

Ted was preparing my dinner in the outhouse. Rajah had already got his and his stainless steel bowl was scraping noisily on the concrete floor as he cleared up the last morsels.

Ted seemed to be taking an age to do mine today. He was mixing it more thoroughly than usual. Certainly more than is necessary as far as I am concerned. Very slowly, very tantalisingly, he stirred while he looked down at me. Several times I got excited and jumped up in the hope of speeding things up a bit. He pushed me down. I half whined, half squeaked to hurry him. 'I'm hungry.' 'Good girl Bess, speak.'

I backed off a pace and barked. Ted's falsetto voice amazed me as he went into masses of praises. With a great flourish he slid my food bowl towards me. About time too. Rajah had finished his and was hovering for mine. No chance.

Ted did virtually the same thing with my favourite toys. He would hold them high above his head and wave them about. 'Speak Bess Speak.'

When I made some sort of noise, usually out of frustration, he praised me and threw the toy for me. In the end the toy became just his clenched fist as though he had something hidden in it for me. That, accompanied by the word 'speak' was enough to trigger me off.

Seemed odd, me barking at him but, still, if that was what he wanted.

I enjoyed my life. I even liked the training. It was always done in short spells and I never got bored. Each period of work was followed by a great game and plenty of praise.

At eight months old I could track someone who had walked across a field half an hour earlier. I knew what to do when Ted said 'Sit', 'Stand' or 'Down'. I could retrieve most things that he threw for me. We ran through exercises almost daily, whether he was on duty or not.

On more than one occasion, Jan said she thought that I had more than one wife but she understood that any effort put in now would pay off in the future.

Although I was free to do so most of the time, I did not play with Rajah so much any more. Sometimes he was very good and we would play together in the garden but most of the time it ended up with him getting nasty and growling at me before he went and found a quiet corner. Once, when he was lying outside the back door, Jan went to step over him as she had done a thousand times before. He lifted his head and growled at her for no reason at all. Ted shouted at him from inside the house. It seemed that Ted was shouting at him quite a lot these days and I did not like it.

Sometimes at night, I would hear Rajah whimper in the darkness at the other end of the kennel. What was the matter with him?

CHAPTER TWO

Mountbrowne Bound

'How many shirts did you put in, love?' Ted called as he was cleaning my tracking harness and lead with Neats Foot Oil. There was an air of excitement about this Sunday. I could not make out just what it was.

Both Rajah and I had had a long grooming session and we both shone and looked quite a nice pair of Alsatians, apart from my ears of course. All my grooming equipment had been scrubbed and was drying in the sun. The car was cleaned. Jan was upstairs packing a suitcase.

The following morning even more activity took place. What was going on?

Wellington boots were put into the car along with endless supplies of waterproof clothing. Then that huge suitcase. 'Hope there'll be room for me. Hope I'm going, wherever it is.' Sure enough, it was not long before Ted opened the garden gate and I jumped excitedly into the back of the estate car. As I pressed my nose against the side window, I could see Jan standing by the gate. Ted was talking to her as he leaned down to stroke Rajah's ears. He kissed Jan goodbye and we were off. I did not know where to but I knew something was going on. Something very special.

Two hours later we arrived at the Surrey Police Dog Training Centre at Mountbrowne, Guildford.

Ted drove into the car park and stopped under the trees. In the distance I could hear the barking of many dogs, announcing our arrival to the world. There were already several vehicles in the car park and I could see that some of them had dogs in. Wonder if they were as excited as I was?

Ted left me in the car while he went to report in so I had time to have a look around. There was the kennel block where I was to live for the next thirteen weeks or so. There, across the other side of the road, was the wood where Ted and I would spend a lot of leisure time.

He returned to the car and I snaked my head into the inviting check chain. We walked into the large kennel block. 'Here's a kennel, Ted. How about this one? No? There's another. No?' He walked me right to the very end of the block, right away from the door. The very last kennel was vacant and it was to be mine.

I wanted her to be in that one because it avoided all the other handlers having to walk past her kennel at all hours of the day. It was a tip I had picked up from my initial course with Rajah and I knew just how tired the dogs would become in the next few weeks.

Ted got into the kennel and crouched down, stroking me. He knew that it would all seem very strange to me. I could see that although the kennel was clean and smelled of disinfectant, it was old and bore the marks of countless previous occupants.

He hung my lead on the ledge provided and with a last word of encouragement, he left and closed the door. I could hear him outside as he introduced himself and chatted with other course members. I too, added my marks to the kennel door as I jumped up to try to see him.

Very soon there was a commotion in the kennel next to mine. Black and silver in colour. Full of beans and raring to go. He nosed me through the wire and spun round in friendly greeting. All the way from Suffolk, 'Blitz' had arrived!

I was curled up on the boards when I heard Ted at the door taking down the lead. Into the chain and we walked along the corridor past all the other kennels and their occupants. There were dogs who barked at us. There were dogs who looked at us rather sullenly. There were even one or two who barked nervously and then slunk away into the comparative safety of their bed spaces.

I blinked in the sunlight as we left the block. Looking back I could see other handlers coming out with their charges too. We all went into a large compound and joined the line that was forming along one side. I had never seen so many dogs together at one time. If I looked along the line I could see Blitz about four dogs along. I wriggled my bottom forward a bit so that I could get a better look. Ted pulled me back. I leant back so that I could look along the line behind him. Again I was corrected. I was really excited about being here with all these potential friends. I managed to sneak another look along at Blitz to find that he was peering back at me. I liked him a lot.

The voice attracted my attention to the other side of the compound. There stood two men. One of them spoke in a curious accent.

'A right motley bunch we have here. The dogs aren't much better either.'

One by one the handlers, complete with dogs, had to go out to the front to introduce themselves, formally, to the other course members. It was good when it was Ted's turn because then I could see all the other dogs without having to tie myself in knots and risk Ted's wrath. What a mixture they all were. There was not one other with a black shaggy coat and brown feet. I do believe that they all had pricked up ears. I was also the only bitch on the course.

Ted obviously knew several of the men, presumably from previous courses, and the atmosphere was quite relaxed. He finished his introduction and started to make his way back to his place in the line. He was stopped by calls of 'O.K. Ted. A joke's a joke but now get your proper dog out.' I could not help thinking that it might be their dogs that were unusual, but I somehow did not really believe that. I wondered if my ears, by some miracle, would ever stand up.

When all the introductions had been made, we were split into two groups. It was a fairly large intake and we were all at different stages of our training. In fact there were two handlers who did not even have dogs when they arrived, so they were to be allocated to them later in the day. All the dogs that had been introduced to tracking were to be with the instructor with the lilt in his voice. I later learned from another experience that it was a Welsh accent.

The remainder of the afternoon was free so Ted took me for a long walk to get rid of the stiffness of the journey down and to find out about the area. It was beautiful there and the kennel block was high on a hill which gave nice views across the countryside.

It was getting towards tea time when Ted put me back into the kennel with a bowl of fresh water. When he left I had a quick sniff of Blitz's nose through the wire and then I had a nap.

The kennel block became rather gloomy as the sun went down but I soon cheered up when Ted came in with my food bowl. The food was different but it seemed to go just as quickly. Ted picked up the bowl while I was still looking for crumbs. He went away and washed up and then we went for our last walk of the day. This was a gentle stroll because I had just been fed. At eight o'clock Ted put me in the kennel and, after checking that I had ample water, he left me for the night.

I had made myself a rule that Bess would have a twelve hour night. In my efforts to do well on my basic course with Rajah, I had worked him in the evenings and again at weekends if we had a problem. I had overdone it and the dog had rebelled for some time. Bess was well up with her training and I had no need to rush this time.

In actual fact I did not get much sleep that night anyway because handlers were coming and going until late into the night. When the activity did eventually die down, one of the dogs decided to howl because he did not like his surroundings very much. Blitz next door seemed to sleep through it all. I could hear his contented snores punctuated by little whimpers as his active mind reconstructed the events of the day and the runs across fresh pastures. No wonder he had so much energy when he was awake.

The following day, amid great excitement, we were taken out for our first run of the morning. Ted and Blitz's handler seemed to hit it off right away and they walked and talked while Blitz and I ran in the woods and got rid of our pent up energy and of course other necessary things. I hated soiling my kennel or compound and would contain myself if I could. I knew roughly when I would be taken out so it was no problem really. We dogs are creatures of habit you know.

A good run and it was back to the kennels and to the grooming blocks. Ted had great fun watching the newer handlers with their dogs as they tried to get them to stand still to be brushed. I was long past that stage and loved the feel of the brushes on me after Ted had run his hands all over me to look for cuts, thorns and dried mud, etc. The two instructors were there, telling the new boys what to look for and to recognise signs of things that might be amiss.

This was it. All on the leads and down to the field. All to the left of the handler. Some slightly in front. Some lagging behind, but all more or less together, we walked down the hill. Once on the field, we were split into our respective groups.

The Welshman asked the handlers one by one what stage they had reached and we all had a run through of the heelwork.

I somehow knew that this was important to Ted, and I did my utmost to show off well. With my right shoulder against his left knee we did left turns, right turns and about turns. Halts in the sit, halts in the down and stand. We finished and the instructor did not say anything but seemed satisfied with all of us.

That is the benefit of dog and handler being together for some time before the course. The bond should already be formed. Just think of the two men who joined the course without dogs. They had to do what Ted and I had been doing for weeks, but all in a few days, if they could.

Next, the instructor did a very strange thing. While we all stood in a large circle around him, he started jumping about and making threatening moves towards each dog in turn. We were encouraged to be aggressive back at him and to bark. I enjoyed that. 'Go on Ted. Let me go and I'll show him for you.'

There were different reactions from different dogs. Blitz was good and showed a lot of controlled aggression and shouted his head off. Another dog stood there, not sure what to do and probably remembering being told off for doing the self same thing to a postman or some other tradesman, whilst with a previous owner. One dog just backed away and peered through the legs of a somewhat embarrassed handler.

The instructor produced an old sack and came towards me, breaking up his outline by hunching his shoulders and looking suspicious. As he came closer, Ted encouraged me to watch him. Watch him? I could see nothing but this threatening stranger. Let me at him. 'Go on girl. Pas Auf.' The lead went slack and I lunged forward to grip the sacking. I was determined to drag it from the man's grasp. I could not of course, but I had a good try and even tried shaking it to see if that would do any good. Out of the corner of my eye I saw the instructor nod at Ted.

'Good girl. Bess. Leave.' The praising words, the smoothing hands. I knew that I should have let go straight away but I could not resist having one last shake. 'Bess. Leave.' The command was almost barked at me. I let go, spitting out strands of sacking as I did so. This was much the same as the games I had played with Ted, in the garden at home.

That night was a little quieter in the kennel block. Dogs settled more readily after the day's exercise. The howler howled less frequently. Blitz snored, the same as usual. I slept quite well, too.

The following day, after grooming and kennel cleaning, we were all put into a large van with six cages in it. The van was old and it rattled, but it was surprisingly clean and smelled of disinfectant from numerous scrubbings. Blitz was in the cage above mine and he had the occasional scratch at the floor. I do not know why he did it. Perhaps just to let me know that he was up there.

What about my ears?

We pulled into Dunsfold Airfield and there was an unexplainable air of excitement. It was new. It was fresh and the dew made our feet wet. It made other parts wet when we sat too, but who cares?

After receiving our instructions Ted put me back in the van but, by pushing my face against the wire mesh of the cage, I could see what he was doing. He had put a pole in the ground to use as the start of a track. I could even see my tracking harness and line on the ground at the base of the pole, just waiting.

He disappeared from view so I settled down to watch Blitz's handler doing much the same thing but in the opposite direction. Blitz gave the odd squeak and spun round as his master walked further and further away. I know how you felt, Blitz.

I hopped out of the van, automatically putting my head into the check chain hanging from Ted's hand. We walked towards the start pole of the track. He seemed different and apprehensive. He held the lead a little tighter than usual. His voice had changed although he used the same words.

To the pole. Harness on. Line attached away we go. This is easier than Ted has had me do in the past. I could even see his footprints in the dew, and the grass as it was springing back upright where he had trodden it down. The scent was strong and my olfactory senses filled with it. I tried to run but Ted restricted me by laying back on the line. 'Where's it gone?' In my haste I had passed a turn.

33

The pressure on the line increased and I got worried. I lifted my head as Ted stopped the forward motion altogether. I cast left and right. I even circled right round him as his experience told him to stand perfectly still.

'Track on Bessie. Good girl.' His voice was back to normal and he had forgotten that he was under scrutiny for the first time.

There it is. In my haste I had overshot a turn by about fifteen feet. Off we went again, my shoulders hunched against the harness as Ted put on resistance to slow me down.

The line taut and Ted puffing slightly, we safely negotiated another right-angled turn without any problem. 'What will it be at the end? Will it be my ball? A stick? A piece of rag to pull on?' I tracked on, lifting my head once to see Blitz tracking in the distance.

'Track on.' The words came quite firmly, insisting that my head went down again. I put my nose to the ground right away. I was still going so fast that I almost overshot my ball. Harness off quickly and my ball went rushing off across the short grass. Blitz had finished too, and I could hear the elated tones of his handler as he played with him in the distance.

Ted was rolling up my line and clipping it to the harness, when the instructor came over. 'Loads of potential there, Ted. Just a bit too quick for her own good this time.'

I bounded off for a game with Blitz before anyone could stop me.

So the routine of the days started to form. Tracking in the morning. Sometimes on my scent, sometimes on one of the other handlers. Gradually the length of time that the track was left to cool was increased, as well as the distance itself. It was all designed to build up Bess's stamina as well as her tracking ability.

We would also search for property in the mornings. Four white poles were placed to form an area some twenty yards square. Within this area were placed some five or six articles of different materials. Some wood, some plastic, some metal and some cloth. All of varying sizes too, but all had one thing in common. They all smelled of humans!

One by one I had to retrieve them and take them back to where Ted was standing on the edge of the square. Once again this was an exercise I liked because of the amount of encouragement and praise I received. After doing this a few times even the smallest items such as keys or cartridge cases became relatively easy to find and pick up. I had to take them to Ted and sit in front of him until he told me to leave them.

Building searches and manwork were usually left until the afternoon and, again, I loved this work. I particularly liked searching for the hidden 'criminal' when he was in a cupboard or hidden behind a door. Apart from barking to let Ted know that I had found him, I could have a good scratch at the door before I was called out. Oh. I know that was not the object of the exercise but, if Ted was not there, he could not really stop me, now could he?

During the early stages of building searching I disgraced myself. At least in the eyes of the instructor if not Ted.

The instructor had donned his overalls and had gone off into a large derelict building to hide and to act as the criminal. As he left he muttered his usual words. 'Give me a few minutes.' Ted waited and then challenged the building. 'Come on out, mate. The place is surrounded. This is your last chance.'

The check chain was whipped off over my head and I was away, feet slipping on the tiled floor which was covered with leaves and other debris blown in by the wind over the years. I covered the ground floor very fast, perhaps too fast in my youth and enthusiasm. I later learned that whilst searching a building it paid to stop and stand quietly for the odd moment. It is possible to hear the rustle of clothing or the shuffle of an impatient foot and sometimes even an intake of breath from a nervous person. I found myself on an upper floor outside a toilet block of a large dormitory. Rubbish was strewn everywhere, peeling paint hung from the walls and ceiling like streamers. I stopped. The scent was stronger here. By turning my head to one side I could hear the sounds of a person trying to be quiet. The instructor, or criminal, was hidden in one of the toilet cubicles. The door was locked and even though it reached right down to the floor one deep intake of breath confirmed my suspicions. He was here. Now could I get a little closer to him?

The door of the next cubicle was closed but it responded when I nudged it with my nose. It opened enough for me to get in there. The dividing partition between the two cubicles did not reach the floor and there was a gap of about five inches. Just enough in fact, for me to get my muzzle under and grip the ankle on the other side. The instructor yelled óut, more in surprise than in pain, and I ended up with the bottom of the overalls in my teeth. I spat it out and barked to let Ted know where the man was. Shortly, I was on the lead and Ted finished the exercise. 'Come on out, mate,' he shouted to the closed door. A bolt clicked and the door opened. A fairly pale instructor peered round the door to make sure that I was secure. 'Bloody dog. You've got a crafty one there.' Ted made a fuss of me and let me know that he was pleased. Inwardly, I knew that the instructor was happy too, despite the mishap with his overalls.

Who's a Niggly Skipper?

At five o'clock one morning all the handlers were at the kennels. All were trying their hardest not to make a noise but failing miserably as each dog welcomed its master.

This time just a quick run in the woods to relieve the accumulation of the night and then into the big kennel van.

The van pulled into the misty airfield at about six o'clock and the sergeant stopped.

'Take the van round to the other side and wait. Pick me up in forty-five minutes.' He took out all the equipment he needed to lay tracks and then disappeared into the gloom. A course member did as we were told and drove the van to the far side of the airfield. Everyone settled down to wait. The dogs dozed off because there was not much doing, while the men started telling jokes and recounting their experiences with previous dogs. A cup of tea from the flask. More jokes. More stories.

Suddenly the sliding door at the side of the van was torn open by a very irate Welsh sergeant.

'I told you lazy so-and-so's to pick me up.' He went ranting on, when through the wire, I saw Ted reach out and grip the sergeant's cheek between his thumb and forefinger. 'Who's a niggly skipper, then?' Ted said, in a chiding voice.

I did not believe what I had seen and the van went a deathly quiet. It seemed an age before the sergeant's face creased into a grin.

'You sod. How on earth can I give you a rollicking?' Laughter broke out from a van load of very relieved dog handlers. It was a good day after that.

Problems at Home

The days became more and more full as extra exercises were introduced. The obedience was done on our own, first thing in the morning, but then we were with the instructors. It was all quite repetitious really but enjoyable all the same. I know that I was always ready for my dinner at the end of each day, anyway.

The best part of the day for me was in the evening when Ted took me for a nice relaxing stroll, to unwind from the turmoil of the day. He tried to work it so that we were alone. No matter how much trouble we had encountered during the training, Ted managed to put it to the back of his mind so that we started afresh the next day. At some stage during our walk he would make sure that he got down to my level on the ground and we would have a rough and tumble and a great deal of fuss. No work at all, just play and body contact.

Although I never fouled my kennel during the night it was scrubbed out each morning. On a Friday afternoon, after lunch, the whole kennel block and the big vans were scrubbed from top to bottom. Then at four o'clock it was into the car and home for a nice relaxing weekend with Jan and Rajah.

I had also made another rule for myself. No training, other than environmental, for Bess, and more time for Jan and Rajah.

The second weekend when we got home, Jan was waiting at the gate. Although she patted me as I said hello to her, she did not pay me as much attention as usual. Rajah did not greet me at all and did not give Ted his usual welcome either. Something was wrong and Jan was troubled and needed to talk to Ted.

While we were away in Surrey, another handler came by each day to take Rajah out for a run. He was a man who I worked with and Rajah knew him well. For no apparent reason, the dog had turned on the man and had bitten him quite badly. Rajah had also been growling at Jan and had wanted the solace of his kennel most of the time.

Ted made several phone calls that evening and the next day a sergeant arrived to collect Ted and Rajah. I stayed at home with Jan. Was she crying? I did not like that morning at all.

Ted came home just before lunch time and I looked beyond him for Rajah but the back of the van remained closed. Ted was obviously upset as I went to greet him.

'Hello, Bessie,' he said abstractly, and did not even look at me. I knew that something was wrong. His eyes were puffy and red. I followed him into the house, looking over my shoulder but the van still remained closed. Where was Rajah? Jan was in the kitchen. She only looked at Ted and started crying again.

I held her and explained. Rajah had been to see the vet, who had diagnosed a brain tumour which was inoperable. The vet had just increased his anaesthetic and Rajah had gone to sleep peacefully.

The remainder of the weekend was miserable, although I made the most of it. They both seemed to want me around and, apart from the night time, I spent most of the weekend indoors with them. On the Sunday Ted scrubbed out the kennel and when it was dry he moved my bed into the proper bed space which Rajah had occupied. It seemed strange during that night and I missed that cantankerous old dog.

On Monday when Ted and I returned to Surrey, Jan had arranged to go to a friend's house for the day. It would be all right for Ted for he had other things to occupy his mind, but Jan would miss having Rajah around.

Seasons Come and Go

The training became more and more intensive as the course continued. The Initial Dog Course is thirteen weeks long, but when you break it down it is only sixty-five working days and that is without Bank Holidays and handlers' court commitments. Sixty-five days in which to turn out a trained team. There is a lot of pressure on those instructors.

Some exercises I found difficult to pick up, and some I could do very well but decided to play up because I had the devil in me. Ted cajoled me in the first instance and corrected me in the second. When he scolded me it was purely with his voice alone but, believe me, that was enough, and I hated it. I trusted him and knew that he would not make me do anything that might harm me.

Since the course had started, I had done nothing in the way of agility and the other dogs were way in front of me on that exercise.

I was erring on the side of caution because of the operations on Bess's front legs. They had obviously not troubled her during the course and now was the time to introduce her to the agility equipment.

It was made into a game with lots of praise. Ted kept a watchful eye on my joints and frequently felt them to ensure that they were not becoming swollen or inflamed. They did not bother me at all. The only thing that bothered me at the moment was the very strange feeling welling up in my stomach. Strange but not at all unpleasant.

At night in my kennel, I would always sniff Blitz through the wire before we settled down to sleep, only now Blitz did not settle so readily and he stood there looking at me long after I had gone into my sleeping compartment.

Two or three days later, during my grooming session, Ted paid particular attention to my tail and rear end. Bit embarrassing really, with all those dogs looking on so intently. 'Vulva's swollen, Skipper. She's well and truly in season now.'

That night I slept in another kennel away from the other dogs. Ted sprayed me with some stuff that smelled of lemons and I did not like that. I felt like an outcast, and at a time when I wanted to be friendly with everyone. There was more than one dog howling that night, I can tell you!

I was still able to work but Ted was left to his own devices and found training venues away from the other dogs. I missed the odd play times with Blitz and the others, none of whom were feeling much like work, anyway.

Ted's name was mud for days, until my season was completely over.

Waterbaby Again

Ted was extremely pleased with my response to the training for manwork.

I was worried when I opted to work a bitch about the manwork aspects of training. Bitches are renowned for being softer than dogs. They are not as powerful and that leather training sleeve that the 'criminal' wears for protection is very big and bulky. A dog, in the early stages of manwork training, must be allowed to win.

I enjoyed it immensely. I am quite powerfully built, certainly large for a bitch and probably bigger than Blitz. I do not particularly look like a bitch either. My coat, being black and fairly long, gives the impression of size. Of course, this had led to me being called 'An overgrown Collie' and an 'Afghan Hound', but usually in good fun.

One time I really made Ted's day. We marched in a line out of the training centre. I knew that there was to be manwork because I could see that the instructor was carrying the equipment. We walked for about a mile or so and I realised that the instructor was no longer with us. I suddenly also realised that all the other handlers had stopped walking. What on earth is going on? 'Hey you. I want a word with you.'

I got excited at the now familiar challenge, and tone of voice. I did not see him immediately but, yes, there he was, running about a hundred and fifty yards away. 'Come on Ted. Let me go.' He fought to release the chain as I struggled and made it more difficult for him.

'Pas Auf.' The chase command. I raced after the man over the rough ground. 'Hello, this is different.' I had run full speed to the bank of the canal. I leapt into the water, half in enthusiasm, half because my momentum would not allow me to stop.

Twenty yards, then ten. I scrambled up the bank. No time for a shake. 'Ah, there he is.' Back to full speed, leaving a trail of water across the towpath. 'Just you wait 'til I get there.'

I closed my teeth on the proffered arm and hung on. The man's breathing was laboured after his run but he still struggled. My claws dug into the soil as I stopped the man's forward flight. I pulled and pulled and hung on until Ted came puffing up, having found his way across the bridge.

I nearly did not hear the word of command because he was almost laughing with joy. 'Leave, Bess. Good girl,' he blurted out. The instructor smiled. 'No problem there Ted. Smashing.'

I do not know what else the instructor said because I now had time for a good shake, so I did. All over them both.

The hike back to the training centre was highlighted by the comments of the Welshman. 'Huh. Fancy a bitch showing up all these big bold dogs. Afraid of getting their feet wet, were they?' Apparently, I was the only one to complete the chase across the water, the first time.

Dreaded Sendaway

We were two thirds of the way through the course and were well up to schedule with our training. I was thoroughly enjoying this one as there was no pressure on either of us. All the work I had put in before the course was paying off. I was told that I could start the 'Irretrievable Object' and the 'Sendaway'.

Two days later, during my early morning obedience session, Ted made me sit at the edge of the sports field. Telling me to stay, he walked in a straight line out into the middle of the field. What on earth was he doing? He stopped and turned to face me. He waved his hand in the air as though he was holding something and bent down to put it between his feet. He walked back to me. What were we doing? It could not be tracking, I was not in harness. What were we doing?

He crouched down beside me with his left arm over my back so that his hand reached round and stroked my chest. I wanted to get out there to see what he had left behind. 'Good girl. Go away.' The 'away' was emphasised. He released his arm at the same time and I raced away to find out what he had put on the ground. Before I got to the spot where he had stood, he shouted: 'Down, Bess,' very firmly. I went down. 'What is this? I'm not even there yet.'

Ted ran out to me, praising me but making sure that I did not get up to meet him.

I could not make out why I was being praised. I had not done anything. I had not retrieved anything for him. What had I done to make him so happy?

He did the same thing again although this time when he returned from his solo walk across the field he just said, 'Away Bess.' Again the emphasis on the 'Away'. Again I went at full speed towards the spot where he had stood, again I was stopped before I got there. Once more he raced out to praise me. We had a good game and did not do any more of that exercise that day. I was pleased when we went back to the more mundane side of training. At least I understood what that was all about.

We practised the 'sendaway' frequently and I eventually learned that when he said that word, I had to run away in a straight line until he told me to stop. I did not like it at all. For so many months, Ted had been coaxing me to walk nicely by his side and suddenly I was being sent away from him. It was not to chase anyone for him or to take something back to him. Had I done wrong? Did he want to be away from me for a while? I did not understand.

Bring it if You Can

The irretrievable object was a different matter. I have already said how much I like to search for property, and people, if it comes to that. Ted made me sit and stay. He walked away from me. Oh. No. Not the wretched sendaway thing again. He had my check chain with him and he made a great play of hanging it on a low branch of a tree. When he came back I half knew what he would say next.

'Seek and Fetch, Bess.' 'Fetch' was a word that I knew well from my retrieve exercise and I needed no second bidding. I raced forward and snatched the chain from the low branch. No problem. He did the same again but this time it was on a higher branch. Again I charged up to the tree expecting to find the chain as easily as the first time. Where was it?

The scent of Ted was coming down the trunk of the tree. I stood on hind legs and stretched up as far as I could. It was two feet above me. I could see it but no matter how I tried, I could not reach it. I jumped, I stretched. I even scratched at the trunk but that did no good. In the end, out of frustration, I barked.

Well. The amount of praise I got was amazing. Anyone looking on would have thought that Ted had gone completely mad. I guess he was pleased with me. He reached up and grabbed the chain and threw it for me to chase. Again, I was made to sit while he walked off with it. I was enjoying this and I managed to gain a couple of feet by wriggling my bottom forward. He did not see. 'Seek and Fetch.'

I was at the bottom of the tree before he even finished the words. Now. Where is it? I could not see it but I remembered smelling it down the tree trunk last time, so I tried there. Nothing. I stood still for a moment, looking for Ted. I was not sure what to do.

'Seek and Fetch.' The emphasis on the 'Fetch' again. I started searching, triggered by the familiar word. 'Good girl,' came the gentle encouragement.

Wait a minute. I was down wind of a pile of house building bricks. Yes. It was there somewhere. I scratched and a brick moved, releasing more scent. I heard the chink of the chain as it moved deep down in the brick pile. Try as I might, I could not get it out of there. I stood back and looked at Ted, willing him to come and get it for me. He did not move. 'Seek and FETCH.'

A tentative scratch to see if the chain would miraculously free itself from its prison. A bark of frustration. A whoop of delight from Ted. 'Oh. So that's what he wants is it?' Another bark. 'Yes. Good girl.'

I barked some more. Again great praise as he came forward to retrieve my chain and send it spinning through the air with a great flourish. Ted was pleased. I was happy.

We did no more of that exercise during the day, but in the coming weeks we practised it a lot. Sometimes it was my chain. Sometimes it was my red ball stuck somewhere where I could not reach it.

Eventually it became a large heavy piece of metal which was just lying in the open. I could not resist having a scratch at it, just in case I could pick it up, before I stood back and barked to tell Ted where it was. He came forward more slowly now and kept me barking longer. He always picked it up and moved it a few yards no matter how heavy it was. After all, what was the point of me finding something and telling him where it was, if he was just going to leave it there?

The metal object is supposed to represent a stolen safe or anything similar that Bess could not carry back to me.

So the training continued. Every day a little different now. Strange areas to track in. Different people's scents but always human scent. I was discouraged from the temptation to track on the scent of other dogs, foxes or rabbits. There were articles of various materials to be found on my tracks. Weapons to be found and retrieved. Ted taught me to lie down beside them when I found them.

They would then be preserved for forensic examination later.

Testing Time

It was a Thursday when I was taken for my first walk much earlier than usual. On returning Ted groomed me especially well until my, perhaps somewhat scruffy, long coat fairly gleamed. He polished up my lead and I noticed that attached to it was a brand new shiny, check chain. 'No chance of a quick throw of that one I suppose?'

When the prolonged grooming session was complete, he put me back into the kennel. This in itself was unusual because we normally went training straight after that period.

About an hour later Ted was back along with the other handlers. They all looked extremely clean and tidy with boots polished and uniforms neatly pressed and brushed. I had a feeling that they would not stay like that for very long, once we welcomed them again. Although Ted and the others were laughing and joking as usual, I could sense a different atmosphere. I think they were nervous!

All dogs and handlers were marched to the field. As it came into view I could see that someone had been very busy since I was last there. The grass was freshly cut. The agility equipment had been moved so that it was right in front of rows of seats which had appeared in front of the pavilion.

After thirteen weeks of training, this was our Pass Out. The rows of seats were filling up with dignitaries from various police forces in the region. All Chief Constables of each course member were invited. Some supported their dog sections, some did not. It was also policy to invite the previous owners of all the dogs to come and see how their former charges had turned out. Some came.

Some did not. This would not apply to Bess because I had got her directly from her breeder. I counted myself very lucky about this because some of the handlers had arrived with mature dogs who had already developed many faults and bad habits which had to be identified and cured before any progress could be made.

The running order for the test had been pinned up on the notice board. Blitz was third to go on, we were fifth which pleased me a lot.

The first seven dogs were kept in the area of the field while the remainder were sent back to the kennels to await their turn.

'Come on. Let's get this thing over and done with.'

I could not see the first four dogs perform as both Ted and I had to keep out of the way. After what seemed a life-time we were called. It was our turn at last. This was what we had worked so hard for, for so many weeks.

'Here we go Bessie.' We walked briskly out onto the field from behind the pavilion, eager to get on, now that our time had come. Ted was talking to me all of the time. 'Must be nerves. Mustn't let him down.'

We walked to the man who was standing alone on the field. We stopped in front of him and Ted made me sit. He saluted and introduced himself and then me — Bowesmoor Wynne — had not heard that in a long time. The man wrote something on his clip board. Another man came up.

This was the steward and he would be giving all the instructions from now on. I knew him from the distant past and his jokes eased the tension somewhat. Why was I so uptight? Bess was well up to this. I hoped I would not let her down.

The steward became serious and Ted settled me on the mark indicated and adjusted my chain so that it was nice and loose around my neck. 'Normal pace, forward,' came the command. We were away. Ted strode off in an exaggerated striding pace. I walked beside him trying to keep my right shoulder against his left knee as we had done on countless occasions in the past. The lead and chain hung loosely under my neck, the lead across Ted's body and into his right hand.

'Turning to the left. Left turn.' Ted gave a sharp intake of breath and I knew that the turn was coming. His right leg swung across in front of me as he changed direction. 'In the stand. Halt.'

'Stand.' Ted drew out the word as we halted.

'Lead and chain off now please.'

Ted removed the equipment and handed it to the steward. I could not resist having a quick look to see where my chain was off to.

'Double pace forward,' came the order.

With his hand up to stop his hat falling off, Ted started forward.

'Heel, Bess.'

I think I must have been day-dreaming because I was a bit slow off the mark and lagged behind a little.

'Right turn.'

Ted marked time momentarily while I caught up. He was not happy.

The remainder of the heelwork went off alright. I lost the odd mark or two but it was not too bad. Ted gave me a good pat while we made our way to the agility area. We were still under scrutiny so I could not leap about as much as usual.

Six foot scale first. Ted positioned me beside him and told the steward that we were ready.

'In your own time, carry on.'

'Bess. Get up.' Ted almost lifted me with his voice. I launched myself at the top edge of the scale. There was no purchase and I slipped for an instant. My front feet were over the top edge and I hauled myself over. Groans came from the crowd as they thought I was going to fall back. Pause for an instant to gather myself for the drop to the other side. I hit the ground and turned to await the recall.

'Bess. Get up.'

Again I leapt for the top on the return journey. I landed and walked the two paces to sit in front of Ted.

'Exercise finished,' said the steward.

'Bess. Heel.' I spun round Ted to sit on his left, nuzzling my nose in his welcoming left hand, as usual. The praise and the pat.

Next. The three foot hurdle with its loose bar at the top, designed to fall at the slightest touch. I cleared it well. Just the long jump to do and agility will be over. The long jump. Five little hurdles spread out to cover nine feet. Ted positioned me about thirty feet before the first segment of it.

'Go on, girl. Get up.' His voice raised abnormally to give me the impetus to clear all parts of it. I skidded to a halt on the far side of the apparatus and waited until Ted joined me. He stood to attention beside me.

'Exercise finished.' Three paces forward then explode into play. Still not too much though. We still have more work to do.

The obedience round was over and we had not done too badly. I lost some marks on the speak on command when my attention was drawn to someone in the crowd opening a packet of crisps. Ted had to give an extra command. Well, it was a long time to dinner!

I was walked over to the two white poles about six feet apart, creating an imaginary line between them. Ted got me into position. This was the long down exercise.

'Down,' he shouted. 'Stay.' I had never heard him shout a command like that before. It must have been his nerves. I stayed there, my attention torn between the corner of the pavilion around which Ted had disappeared and the performance of the next dog on the field. My heart sank as the dog failed the scale and fell back at the feet of his handler.

'We must be well into the ten minutes by now. Where's Ted? I must turn over to get off this hard lump in the ground. Shouldn't lose any marks for that. Ah, that's better.'

A few minutes later the steward went to the corner of the pavilion and reappeared with Ted.

Ready for Pass-Out

44

I had just gone through the longest ten minutes of my life.
Ted approached. His eyes were fixed on a point way beyond me. No eye contact or I might get up to greet him and the exercise was not over yet. I could feel him willing me to stay there and not to get excited at his return. Involuntarily, my tail moved from side to side. We had done this so many times before but this time it seemed so important to get it right.

'Exercise complete. Nice round, Ted. Well done.'

Ted called me up into the sit position and then we moved quickly off the arena so as not to disturb the dog still working.

When we were out of sight behind the pavilion, we had a whale of a time. We had put on a good performance and he let me know it.

Several people came round to talk to Ted and I received a lot of fuss from them too. We had to remain in the arena until the last dog had completed its obedience round, then it would be the steadiness to gunfire test. First, there was time to examine the scoreboard to see how things were going. At least Ted did. I just sat beside him with his hand fussing my ear while he scrutinised all the figures. Blitz was doing well and we were right up there with him.

'Handlers,' came the call.

All those in the first group lined up for the gun test. We were walked in line abreast away from the steward, who, when we were about twenty yards from him, fired the first shot. I automatically looked over my shoulder for a criminal. The dog to my right spun round his handler but was quickly brought under control. I heard Blitz, along the line, having his say.

'About turn.' Once again the gun went off as we approached the judge and steward. Commands of 'Heel' came along the line though I suspect that some were unnecessary. All dogs stayed under control and we all marched off to a ripple of applause. Comments were passed between onlookers and those people who laid claim to having brought up such obedient dogs before giving them to the police!

'Just a Minute!'

'When you are ready Ted, we'll crack on.' The steward stood beside Ted. Apart from us and the judge who was standing a few yards away, the arena was empty. Or was it? 'What's that man doing over there? Ah. It's manwork!'

'Challenge him now,' hissed the steward.

Ted's voice caught in his throat. 'Stay Bess. Just a minute. I want a word with you. Don't run. Stand still.' It came out as a bellow.

'Send her, then,' said the steward.

'Pas Auf.' Ted had hardly got the first of the German words out and I was gone. I had eyes only for that man with the odd looking run, going across the field. I went as fast as I could, narrowing the angle to cut him off.

There was the arm. Another two paces to adjust. A leap and the arm was mine. The man gasped as my eighty-five pounds hit him hard. He fought to keep his feet as my momentum overtook him. The taste of the covering sleeve and the bulky leather padding were very familiar by now. I tightened my grip and saliva formed. My feet made scores on the ground as I dug in to stop the man's forward flight.

All too soon, Ted came running up, closely followed by the steward.

Ted shouted at the man. 'O.K. Mate. Stand still, Bess, leave him.'

The man stood still and I let go of his arm and went to Ted's side. 'Down and Stay.'

I dropped into the down position. Ted left me and walked in an exaggerated semi-circle to emphasize that he would not get between me and the criminal.

'Turn and face the dog. Feet well apart. Arms up. Now stand still.' I think Ted frightened the man himself but I gave a few barks to make sure that he knew that he was not going anywhere.

From behind the man, Ted searched him thoroughly to make sure that he was not armed with anything. He then walked back to me, again demonstrating that he would not get in the way of my line of sight of the criminal. When he rejoined me he told the man to walk towards the judge. I walked about six paces behind him, hoping all the time that he would try to get away again, but he did not. 'Right. Halt.' We arrived at the judge who said, 'Exercise finished.' I had another good pat from Ted as he thanked the 'criminal'. I was very glad to see him rubbing his wrist as he walked away.

The steward called Ted to him but as we walked I could not resist another look over my shoulder at the receding leather sleeve.

'Right Mate, Stand still. I want a word with you.' The familiar challenge. I looked to where the first criminal was standing with the judge. No. He's not doing anything.

Then I saw him. Another man was running across the field, taking the same route as the first. 'Send him,' said the steward.

Ted had barely muttered the command and I was gone. It did not even bother me that the steward had called me a 'him'. This man was not running quite as fast as the first man had, and he kept looking over his shoulder towards me. There was something different about this. Suddenly, I found out why. I was bearing down on the man when he stopped and turned and faced me, his hands clasped in front of his body. 'Stand Off!' The temptation to bite was great. The momentum of my run. The grass still slippery. I slid and collided with the standing man. He gasped as some of the wind was knocked out of him.

I moved away from him and started barking at him. A quick look for Ted who was puffing across the field, again followed by the steward. Another bark at the man to make sure that he did not move.

As he arrived, Ted called me out and I went to his side. He told me to stay and went to talk to the man and ascertained that he was innocent. He then allowed him to walk back to the judge.

I stood there fussing Bess's ear and trying to look nonchalant but also listening to pick up any of the conversation between the judge and the 'criminal'. I saw the man indicate how slippery the grass was with his foot. He also showed the sleeve of his coat to the judge.

The judge called us over and told me that he was satisfied that there was no bite but a collision.

Ted was over the moon with delight. We had worked hard on the stand-off exercise and he knew that I could do it. I obviously lost a lot of marks because I should have circled the man while I barked at him. Nonetheless, Ted had expected to lose the lot but, after all, this was only a pass out test and not The National Police Dog Championships. You would not have thought so to see those nervous handlers!

The 'stick attack' is probably the shortest of the manwork sequences and yet I enjoy it the most. Timing has got to be just right or I could be hit by that swinging stick. I hung on to the sleeve like mad while Ted disarmed the man by taking the stick from him. I was called out and it was all over.

The gun went off for the final test of courage. The man just stood there, firing the pistol towards Ted as I bore down on him. Across the lessening ground the acrid smell of the smoke filled my nostrils, then I had the man on the wrist, just above the gun. The padding is thin there to allow him mobility. He called out in pain and raised his left arm, the accepted signal that something is wrong. Ted called me off straight away, as he raced in. He praised me because I had done the job for which I had been trained but I had also hurt a colleague. He would be bruised for a few days but that was all. We were standing in front of the judge again.

'Very nice, Ted. Very nice round altogether.' Ted thanked him, saluted, and we walked off towards the pavilion. This time the applause was prolonged. Ted raised his hat in mock salute to some of the course members. I knew that he was very pleased with our performance, so was I.

If Only Time

The ten minute walk back to the kennel block was good. There were just the two of us and we were away from the pressure of the competition for a while. Ted chatted to me most of the way. He was very pleased with the way that we had worked together and it all boded well for the future, when we returned to our own area in the Medway Towns of Kent.

Very soon he was settling me down with a lot of praise, but, more importantly, a bowl of fresh water. He left me in the kennel and went back to watch the progress of the other dogs. I could not stay on the field because the gunfire would excite me and that would not be fair to the other teams that were still working. Anyway, I did not mind. I would enjoy a quiet snooze after my efforts.

Sometime later, the usual hectic period of feeding took place. Dogs got excited as they anticipated the arrival of food bowls.

The score board for the pass out competition had been moved from the pavilion up to the kennel office. Handlers hovered outside the door, awaiting

S U R R E Y   C O N S T A B U L A R Y

POLICE DOG TRAINING SCHOOL

INITIAL COURSE

FROM   8th May   **TO**   5th August

NAME   Police Constable 3476 WRIGHT   **FORCE**   KENT

NAME OF DOG Bowesmoor Wynne (Bess)   **DATE TAKEN OVER** September 1971

GENERAL HANDLING

A good experienced handler who knows what he wants from the animal and
how to obtain it.

OBEDIENCE

Excellent. The dog reacts favourably to this work and shows off well.

TRACKING

Excellent. This is one of the dogs best exercises. She is doing everything
correctly and all that is now required is to push her ahead on older tracks. Shows
great promise at hard surface tracking.

MANWORK

Excellent. Shows plenty of courage and has the right temperament for this
work. Not a very hard biter, but this will improve with age and experience.
Has been introduced to stick and gunfire work.

GENERAL REMARKS

P.C. Wright has had a very successful course. He has worked most conscientiously
and has set a very high standard to the other members of the course. On the end
of course test he came top with 281 marks out of a possible 300. The dog gives
every indication at this stage of training that it should do well in competitive
work.

SERGEANT INSTRUCTOR

OFFICER IN CHARGE

48

the last of the marks to be telephoned through and entered on the scoresheet by a very harassed marker.

Ted was with me as I finished my food. Another handler came in to find him and proffered his hand.

'Well done, Mate. You and that hairy bitch of yours really showed us the way.' Ted took my bowl to wash it up but I knew that he would go straight to the scoreboard afterwards.

There was an atmosphere among the handlers. One of excitement mixed with anti-climax. It was the time for 'If Onlys'. 'If only he hadn't fluffed the scale. If only he had been better on the heelwork. If only he'd got a couple of extra marks for this or that.'

Food bowls emptied and washed up. Water bowls filled with fresh water for the evening. Dogs being given a quick walk before being settled down.

The handlers left for an evening which differed from the rest because I could hear loud music and laughter coming from the accommodation block.

When Ted and some of the other handlers came to give us our last run of the evening, it was much later than usual. As we barked excitedly to welcome them, there were exaggerated 'Shhhhh's' and 'Quiets', accompanied by a lot of giggling and stifled laughter. I suspected that it was not just the handlers' spirits that had been bubbling this night.

The following day spirits were not quite so high and a few headaches were complained about. Nonetheless, the handlers were all clean and tidy ready for a presentation by the Assistant Chief Constable. This day we were all allowed to walk on the immaculate lawns outside the headquarters complex.

'Form up on Ted,' called the instructor, and a lot of shuffling and changing of places went on.

'Parade, Shun.'

The handlers all stood up straight. The dogs, while sitting beside them, looked left and right along the line, and at the man approaching. He came up to Ted and me.

'P.C. Wright. Kent. Sir,' snapped Ted.

'Congratulations, P.C. Wright. I'm afraid I missed your performance as I was at a meeting but I understand that it was very good. I hope that we'll see you back here in competition.' Ted accepted the certificate and ceramic tile with the Dog School emblem emblazoned on it.

The man then moved on to the next handler and said much the same thing. I reckon that these meetings of theirs are too convenient!

We stood there for ages and a sidelong glance along the line told me that some dogs were finding it more comfortable in the 'down' position.

'Parade, fall out.' At long last.

No work today. We were given a long walk across the fields. Blitz and I played together while the two handlers exchanged addresses and telephone numbers. None of us realised that we would not see each other again.

When we got back to the kennels I was put straight into our car. Ted and the other men set to and scrubbed the kennel block from top to bottom and then did the same to the big vans. It was quite light-hearted and I saw Ted get soaked by a wayward hosepipe.

Soon, everything was clean and tidy for the next lot of novice dogs. Listen to me. Novice dogs! We had just passed out as police dogs and our average age was thirteen months!

A little while later, the handlers returned but this time they were not in uniform and were struggling with bulging suitcases and carrier bags which they loaded into their cars. I watched through the window as Ted shook hands with the two instructors and thanked them again.

They would both start another course on Monday, with a new lot of students and a new lot of problems.

We were then off and I watched the Mountbrowne kennel block, which had been my home for so long, recede into the distance. We were off to a completely different life now.

It was a strange journey home. Ted did not talk to me as much as usual and I could sense he was feeling a bit low. In later life I came to realise that no matter how well we did in trials and competitions, he always had a feeling of anti-climax.

We broke our journey to see the veterinary surgeon who had operated on my shoulders. She was very pleased when Ted told her that we had come top of the course by such a large margin and that I had suffered no ill effects after the agility. She felt my joints all over and moved my limbs about. She was quite happy too.

When we resumed our journey, Ted seemed in higher spirits and did not even seem to mind when I quietly climbed over onto the back seat to be closer to him. It was more comfortable too, I might add.

CHAPTER THREE

Stitch Up

Jan made us very welcome when we arrived home. She knew that life would now settle down to near normality again and that I would not be away for weeks at a time.

That evening after all the unpacking was done and they eventually sat down, I crept in and curled up behind Ted's chair. I think that he, too, was glad that the course was over.

Ted was due some leave and it started that day, but on the Monday we went to our local vet's. Once again I would have another bald patch where the hair was cut away to receive the needle.

'Good girl, Bessie.' Ted's voice seemed so far away and soft, as I felt tired and lay down.

I do not remember much after that until I opened my eyes and found that I was in the kitchen at home. I was on a blanket in the middle of the floor. Jan was wiping my mouth with cool water. My stomach hurt a lot and felt very tight. I lifted my head to see what was causing the discomfort but Ted kept my head firmly to the blanket and I went to sleep again.

The next time I opened my eyes, I was in darkness. I could hear the murmur of the television coming from the lounge. I tried to stand but in doing so, fell against a chair which banged into the kitchen cabinet. Ted appeared and the light came on. He made me stay where I was and brought me some water which I lapped gratefully. My stomach felt numb and I looked to see the fine line about three inches long. The stitches were tight and tinged with blood. I had a quick lick before Ted stopped me.

I did not know it but I would never have puppies. I had been spayed.

The next day I did not feel too bad. My stomach hurt a bit but I felt like moving about and wandered around the garden with Ted as he realised how much work he had to do following the course. The garden was in a bit of a state but he had a week off and would soon get it sorted.

We went out the next day but I was kept on the lead. The stitches were to stay in for a week but I felt better after a couple of days. My stomach had stopped hurting and I wanted to get back to normal with our long walks.

First Night Nerves Dispelled

Ted's leave finished the day before my stitches were due to be taken out, and we were on night duty.

As he prepared for the shift I could sense that he was apprehensive. What would we encounter on our first night out together? How would I react to operational conditions? Would the stitches be all right?

Come ten o'clock and we were rolling down the drive. Ted used the radio to book on watch as available for calls. The anonymous voice crackled back at him and made some quip about him having been on extended holiday and welcomed him back. If only these people knew how hard it is.

It was not a particularly busy night. Ted went to a domestic dispute and helped out at the scene of a road traffic accident but neither time was I taken out of the van.

During the early hours Ted laid me a short training track through the industrial estate. Hard surface — much more difficult than the grass tracks I had on the course, particularly with the breeze getting up. I found the toy gun that he had used as the last article for me to find and we only had a gentle game because of my stitches.

'Vehicle crashed, person made off.' The radio crackled into life as we got back into the van. The incident was a long way off our area but the local dog handler was already engaged in an incident.

I could sense the adrenalin flowing through him.

We sped towards the Crown Point Inn, Sevenoaks, where the accident had occurred. We arrived to find that a small sports saloon car had left the road and had hit a tree head on. There were several police cars there and an ambulance was also standing by.

'Come on girl.' Ted's voice cracked slightly as he opened the rear doors of the van. Almost in one movement he had me on the chain and my tracking equipment was hanging over his shoulder. We picked our way through the broken glass which crunched under Ted's feet. He stood up as he clipped on the thirty foot line. I went forward, nose down, conditioned by the sight and feel of the harness. Must get on with the work.

There was debris and glass everywhere. There were lots of scents around too, where the police officers had walked as they examined the wrecked car.

Ted moved me away a bit, gently casting me in a semi-circle around the front of the car. This time, the ground was not fouled up with human scents. The dew was heavy. Trails of snails could be seen shining in the moonlight. Rabbits and foxes had passed this way too, but that was not what I was here for although the temptation was great.

I kept working, guided almost unnoticeably by Ted, in that arc, keeping well away from the car. What was that? Another quick check. Yes that was it and I could even see the breaks in the dew. I almost dragged Ted off his feet, the tracking line must have burned his fingers. Through the trees and down the rough bank. A broken fence at the bottom and there was a concentration of human scent. Without thinking I lay down and waited as Ted came sliding down the bank. His torch flashed on and there was a man's shoe. I had not realised it but Ted had been joined by the local dog handler who had finished his other task.

'There's blood on this,' Ted said. 'Track on, Bess.' I was up and tracking before he got the last word out. Ted did not use his torch much as the scent took us out into the disused allotments. A turn to the left and I could see the lights of the police vehicles as the officers tried to extricate the crashed car from the tree.

We had gone some considerable distance. Suddenly, there he was. The scent had become very strong. It was mixed with the sweet aroma of blood and another scent that I did not recognise. The man had crawled under a bush in a very unsuccessful attempt to hide. When Ted switched on the torch, the man was grinning stupidly. There was blood everywhere, from the cuts on his face but the majority of it was coming from where his eye used to be. The eye would be no use to him any more. Perhaps it was a good job that the man had drunk so much whisky because he was oblivious to pain at that moment.

Ted took off the harness and rolled up the line. I jumped around excitedly for this was where I got my game. No. Not this time, it was onto the lead as Ted and the other handler half dragged, half carried the drunken man back to the waiting ambulance and he was taken away.

Ted made me lie down and rolled me onto my side. He shone the torch and examined my stitches closely. 'Your're fine, Bessie boots. Good girl.'

I could tell that he was very pleased with my performance that night and he teased the other handler about not being able to look after his own patch and just to call if he needed help any other time. It was all in good fun though and the other man conceded that Ted's 'hairy doormat' had done quite well for her first night out, considering the stitches and all!

As we drove back towards our own area and home, the sun was coming up. Ted drove slowly and talked to me all the way. I dozed.

When we got home, Ted gave me a drop of milk and I stayed in the kitchen while he had a cup of tea before going to bed. He took me out to my kennel and as I snuggled down in my bed of shredded paper, I knew that if Jan was awake when he went in, she would share in our success, as she would, in the forth-coming years, share in our failures, too.

Ted was up early and we went to the vet's. Ted considered him a friend and as the stitches were removed he related the events of the previous night, obviously very proud of me. The vet felt me all over with sure hands and agreed even if I did not look quite right, I was still strong and healthy. What about these stupid ears?

Just in Time

On the last night of that week we attended a domestic dispute to back up the local '999' car. I had not been called but as I was in the area I popped along to see if we could help out. A lady met me when I arrived. She and her common law husband had argued and he had stormed out of the house and into the rear garden. She later realised that several bottles of pills were missing and, as he had attempted suicide before, she called for assistance.

While the crew of the other car were talking to the lady to get more details, Ted took me out into the garden to search the outbuildings and numerous sheds. 'Go seek, Bess.' I raced off, pleased to have something to do. I checked the outhouses and sheds. I even searched the greenhouse but nobody had been in that for a long time. Right down to the bottom of the garden, I ran. Suddenly, I caught something on the breeze. I stood on hind legs to check the top of the wall. Yes. Someone had gone over there. Ted came forward with his torch on. He checked the top of the wall. Fresh scratch marks. Broken cobwebs. 'Down Bess. Stay.'

He left me in the darkness and ran off to the side gate of the house. When he returned he had my tracking harness and line with him. I refrained from getting up until he got back to me, but only just. He called me up into the 'sit', and then to him at the wall. Shining his torch at the top of it, he said, 'Up, Bess.' I launched myself at the top of the wall and Ted supported my hindquarters. No trials now, so he can help me. As I hit the ground on the other side, he called. 'Down Bess.' As I lay down, I could not resist stretching my neck so that I could sniff the ground in front of me. I had seen the tracking equipment so I knew what was coming.

Ted clambered over the wall and put the harness on me. The excitement mounted as I already knew that there was a track there. Come on, Ted. Get that line on me. Let's go! 'Good girl. Track on.'

The words were wasted as I needed no further bidding than the presence and feel of the harness. The ground was moist and the scent was still fairly strong even though it was well over an hour old.

The ruts cut by a tractor's wheels posed no problem as we turned off across the field. In front of me I could see the lights of the Kingsnorth Power Station reflected in the River Medway.

After about a mile, the scent became stronger. We were going along the river bank, which was a bit eerie in the blackness. Ted never used his torch much. The man was sitting on the river bank. In the light of the torch he looked rather grotesque, just sitting there with his knees drawn up close to his chest and his arms around them. Even when Ted spoke to him, he made no movement.

'Down, Bess,' Ted said, quietly, as he unclipped my line. He went up to the man and shone his torch right into his face.

Ted grabbed the two empty pill bottles from the grass and rammed them into his own pocket. He dragged the man to his feet and with his arm round him to support him, they made their way back across the fields. Once again, I had no game having worked for him.

Before long Ted had the man over his shoulder in a fireman's lift where he got a very rough ride. Ted was puffing and blowing by the time he reached the house and could barely tell the '999' crew what had happened.

'No time for an ambulance. Just get him to the Medway Accident Centre.' He gave them the empty pill bottles and the car sped away. I watched fascinated as the little blue light faded away into the distance.

Ted sat on the wall to get his breath back and to make a fuss of me. About time too.

I called in at the Medway Accident Centre later that night to see how the man was. The Sister on duty told me that he would not have been alive now but for the early treatment.

He eventually spent three nights in the hospital before being sent home.

What you people won't do!

Tomato Ketchup?

In early years, each Saturday was taken up with demonstrations and displays at fêtes or garden parties.

The same dogs and handlers would turn out to do their bit and it seemed to go down well with most people and did a lot to foster good relations with the public.

My favourite part was when, in the finale, I had to attack the man who was armed with a stick. Invariably, I would go in so hard that the man was knocked off his feet. Ted taught me so that when the man fell I would go and take the stick from his hand and take it to Ted, thus disarming the man completely. Although this was only for demonstration purposes, it was liked by most and earned me lots of attention when the people came to talk to the handlers after the show.

Ted said he would like a penny for every person who asked him what breed I was. At one such demonstration at an infants school, all the children were standing safely within the tennis courts, looking through the wire fence so we were able to perform right up close to them.

Ted sent me after the man armed with a gun. One shot. Two shots and through the smoke, I had him. I must have missed my footing or something because I bit him very hard on the unprotected hand that held the gun. Blood poured and Ted called me out as soon as he realised what had happened. One sweet little girl from the rapt audience said. 'Coo. Don't they make it realistic?'

I think it was the same young lady who later came up to Ted and said 'Excuse me. Don't you think that they should bring back hanging?' I think that it was the only time I have ever seen him lost for words.

I was involved in my very first display when I was only fourteen weeks old. Rajah and the other team members had gone through their paces at the Cheshire Homes at Tunbridge Wells. To end the display all the dogs were marched in file around the arena so that spectators could have a closer look at them. On this occasion Rajah was left in the van and I took his place at the end of the line. I was not even used to a lead by this time but the 'Oohs' and 'Aahs' from the audience as I tried to keep up with the big dogs were quite nice.

What I did not like was the ignominy of the 'L' plates that Ted had saddled me with before we joined the team. Still, it amused him and the crowds and I

I win another admirer

(Courtesy of 'Chatham, Rochester & Gillingham News')

received so much fuss when the people came round the van to talk to the handlers. I had my picture taken quite a few times that day.

Later, when I was a fully fledged member of the team we had completed yet another display at a fête in the Medway Towns.

At the time, Jan was in All Saints Hospital and one of the handlers light-heartedly suggested that we should go en masse to visit her while we were in the area. Another suggested that while we had all the equipment with us we could put on another display.

There was quite a commotion as six dog vans drove into the car park at the end of the hospital block. I went in to tell Jan what we were going to do and the balconies started to fill at the end of the multi-storey building. Nurses scurried about moving beds to vantage points. All the patients that could, made their own way to get a better view.

We then carried out our impromptu and abridged demonstration of heelwork, agility and even manwork albeit without the gunfire.

That audience was every bit as appreciative as the previous one that day. Ted and his colleagues probably broke every rule in the book as far as the police were concerned but it was a lovely way to brighten the patient's day and did a great deal for public relations.

A Clean Pair of Heels

'Bravo Charlie Nine. Will you meet the panda car at the building site in Rochester High Street?'

'Received. E.T.A. three minutes,' Ted answered the tinny voice of the controller.

As he stopped the van, the local officer pulled in behind him. A man stepped out of the shadow of a doorway to meet them.

I slipped out of the van as Ted held the door open and put my head into the check chain. I sat there as the man told the two officers what he had seen.

'Two men, with plastic tubing and cans, went behind the generators over there. They are still somewhere on the site. This is the only way out.'

The other officer made the unnecessary comment: 'I reckon that they are nicking fuel but I don't fancy going out into that lot.'

Sure enough, even from where I was sitting, I could see the large muddy puddles on the building site reflecting the surrounding street lamps. 'Let's just try something before we go out there,' Ted said. 'Bess. Speak.' I was taken by surprise and did not do anything. 'Bess. Speak.' It came firmly this time and I was ready for it. O.K. If that's what you want. I let fly. 'Good girl. Speak on,' Ted said, quietly. Then he shouted. 'Right you two. Come on out or I'll send this dog in.' The tone of voice and the now familiar challenge, incensed me to bark even more. Suddenly, it happened. A voice answered from the depths of the building site.

'Keep that f---ing dog on a lead. We're coming out.' Into the lights of the street lamps came two muddy figures, still carrying their plastic tubes and cans.

The officer with Ted could hardly contain himself and tried hard to stifle his amusement as he went through the formalities of the arrest.

Ted just made sure that the muddy pair were taken to the police station in the panda car. He did not want our van messed up! The witness just stood there and said 'Amazing. They ought to get more of them.' He gestured to me. 'Been telling them that for years, Mate. 'Night and thanks again.'

Close Shave

We came on nights at ten o'clock. A quick drive through the towns to make sure that everything was quiet and to let the local beat officers know that we were around. The public houses were busy but there was no trouble yet. We parked up by the Chatham Town Hall. It was Ted's favourite spot because it was busy there, but it was also handy for getting to any other part of the conurbation. A taxi driver pulled up and had a chat with Ted. They got around a lot and saw things that they felt would be of interest to him. Ted was standing on the footpath talking to the driver. 'Bravo Charlie Nine.' It was us. Ted reached in through the open window. 'Go to the Nursery, Lower Rainham Road.' We were there within minutes.

The local beat officer was there to meet us. He told me that one of the nursery-men had taken a lot of pills and had disappeared from the main house where he lived. No one had any idea where he had gone but they were worried because, although he had not been in trouble for many years, he had a tendency to be violent. I decided that, in the absence of any concrete information, we would search the premises thoroughly before going further afield.

There were many massive greenhouses to do and we started with the one nearest the house. Ted opened the door. 'Seek on, Bess.' I searched each of the greenhouses in turn but nothing. He opened the door to the ninth. This time it was different. As he opened the door and the rush of warm air came towards me I knew that this was the one. Ted knew too, from my attitude. 'Good girl. Seek on then.' I did each aisle in turn, looking on top of the benches and sniffing underneath. 'Where is the blighter, I know he is here somewhere? Along the last aisle. Yes. I've got to be very close.' I came to a place where a lot of sacks had been piled up under the bench. He was definitely here. Now, how to get him out? I jumped up onto the bench and I barked at his scent rising through the slatted working area.

Ted came running up, his torch supplementing the feeble electric lighting. 'What have you got then, Bess?' Not a question but said as praise. I jumped down and pulled at the sacks. 'O.K. Mate. Out you come.' Ted started to pull the sacks off in order to get the man out.

Suddenly the man jumped out and grappled with Ted, the pruning knife in his hand coming very close to him. I tasted salt as I bit into the man's trousers and my teeth grazed his skin. I pulled and the man screamed out. Pain and surprise made him throw the knife down.

The local officer and the nursery owner came running in and the man was subdued very quickly. He was taken away in an ambulance obviously still suffering from his concoction of pills. The local officer went with him.

Ted and I were taken into the main house where the owner made a cup of tea. As he handed it to Ted he pointed at something on Ted's tunic. The breast pocket had been nearly sliced open. The thick leather cover of Ted's pocket book had taken the full force of the pruning knife. Neither of us had realised that the knife had come that close.

Occasionally during day shifts, Ted and I visited that nursery as it had become quite a regular tea stop. The man still worked there and he often made a fuss of me but always mentioned the fact that he did not always like me!

Doctor's Dilemma

There were many times when we were involved in searches for missing people. They were usually elderly persons who had wandered off from their homes or from an institution.

One such search took place at Paddock Wood. An elderly lady had gone missing. Her doctor stated that in view of her age and condition, she could not travel far, in fact, no more than half a mile. A massive search was mounted with all available personnel. Six dogs were drafted into the area. We were joined by concerned local residents from the village.

Ted and I were working in front of a line of officers. We were to search a tract of woodland which was fairly dense and difficult to penetrate in places. Every so often Ted would call a halt and I was given a rest while the officers sprawled on the ground. We went on like this all day, finding nothing unusual. I was glad to have a drink when we burst out of the woods into a farmyard. Even out of a hosepipe that water tasted great.

We searched until dusk and then made our way, rather dejectedly, back to the starting point. Ted opened the back of the van and I jumped in. Before sliding the cage doors across he held my head in his hands and fussed my ears and neck. I really had worked hard for him and he appreciated it.

Other handlers and their dogs drifted back and I could see that they too were tired and the dogs were glad to get into the quiet of their vans for a rest.

Each area searched was crossed off on a large map. The whole area had been covered but there had been no trace of the lady. A further briefing was to be held in order to decide the next plan of action. The doctor was there, most irate because the lady had not been found and insisting that, as she could not have travelled far, the dogs had missed her.

We were still working out our strategy when a radio message was received in the control vehicle. The old, frail lady had been found fit and well, thank goodness.

She had been found wandering on Charing Cross Station, having gone to London to do some shopping!

That was one embarrassed doctor, I can tell you!

The searchers were stood down from the incident and one by one they drifted away, tired but happy that the old lady was well, until only the dog handlers remained.

Each handler took it in turn to hide as a missing person for the other.

It was great when at last it was my turn to search. I rushed around the wood half knowing from the previous dogs baying, that there was someone to find. When I did find the man standing beneath a tree, I really let fly and barked my head off to let Ted know where he was, too...

I had been searching all day and had found nothing but now I had the incentive to do it all again the following day should the need arise.

Elizabeth, Born 1899

Another search took place in Chatham for an old lady who had wandered off from a nursing home one lunchtime.

I saw the inspector in charge and got the necessary information and the lady's description.

We got to the area early and started our task before the police personnel had finished their briefing. It is easier for us to work alone. I searched gardens, alleys, rough ground, sheds and outhouses, but to no avail. Ted spoke to residents of the home, neighbours and passers-by but without any further information forthcoming.

It was about six o'clock and the light was fading fast. I went to the collator of the search and looked at the map of the area and at the shaded parts which indicated where searches had been made.

Some local areas had been allocated to members of the public to do. I told the inspector that Bess and I would have a last sweep through that area before the light failed completely.

There was one alleyway which was separated from the nursing home by a very high wall and access to it was from an adjoining street. Ted walked with me on the lead to the entrance of the alley, only to find it overgrown with brambles. He slipped my chain off.

'Seek on. Bessie,' he said, perhaps a little forlornly. The brambles were extremely thick and nettles grew where brambles did not. Something dragged me on though. The scent coming towards me was different, but it was there. It was faint and I was probably only getting it because the breeze was in the right direction.

Ted could see that I was on to something and began to scramble through the undergrowth. Thorns tore at my coat and occasionally got through to my skin. The scent was getting stronger and I once thought that I heard something, too.

I could hear Ted crashing through behind me, and also getting snagged on the thorns, from the expletives. I left him to follow as best he could.

'Good girl. Bess. Where is she then?' The encouragement came from somewhere in the bushes. 'There she is.' I had come to a clearing with trees. The patch was now clear and I could see the old lady lying across the path in front of me. I barked and the lady moved. The smell of dried urine wafted towards me. It was this smell mixed with the usual human odour, that had first attracted me into that part of the alley. She had obviously been there for some time. Ted came crashing through the remaining brambles, spurred on by my bark, the thorns forgotten in his haste. He got down beside the old lady as he said to me 'Good girl. Get down.' I thought the command was a bit harsh considering the work I had done but he only wanted to make sure that the lady was all right. He spoke to her and the replies came as moans. He used his radio and gave directions to the ambulance men, advising them to gain access through one of the old terraced houses that backed onto the alleyway. When the old lady was taken away, Ted and I made our way, via one of the houses I might add, back to the van. I wanted a drink.

The nursing staff had been informed of the good result and the kettle was bubbling when we got back into the nursing home where my van was. I had milk and biscuits while Ted had a nice cup of tea as he pulled the thorns from himself and me.

I still do not know how that resilient old lady, born in 1899, had got into that part of the alleyway. I do know that she was at the hospital for only a few hours

ALIVE AND WELL

Dog finds missing pensioner

By JOHN HENDERSON

A PENSIONER who spent the night huddled under a bush owes her life to an inquisitive police dog.

The dog "sniffed" out 84 - year - old Elizabeth Sisley as she lay unconscious 27 hours after she disappeared.

Staff at the old people's home where she lives believe the bush had sheltered her from overnight dew and helped to keep her alive, but it had also screened her from human searchers.

Elizabeth went missing from Medway Homes in Balfour Road, Rochester, at about noon on Sunday.

SEARCHED

Staff realised she had gone when they could not find her for lunch, so they quickly called the police. Officers searched around the home for Elizabeth, who cannot walk very well or far.

When she was still missing yesterday, a team of officers went to the area with a police dog which found her in an overgrown alley in Ewart Road, near the home.

She was taken to Medway Hospital for a check up and returned to the home last night.

Today officer - in - charge, Margaret Davis said: "She looks tired, but fit. She hasn't suffered any ill effects — in fact she looks better than she did when she went out.

"We're very grateful that the dog found her. The bush sheltered her but a person would never have seen her there."

62

before she was returned to the nursing home. That was after having spent more
than twenty-eight hours in the open, in October!

Working Trials

Rajah, when he was in his prime, had won many Working Trials certificates. We
had travelled far and wide to enter civilian Dog Trials and I thoroughly enjoyed
this hobby. I had great admiration for other competitors from all walks of life
who held down full time jobs and yet still made time to train and compete with
their dogs. There was a great camaraderie and friendly rivalry between these men
and women whose aim was to qualify in each stake and perhaps even get their
dogs to the top by making them a Working Trials Champion. Comparatively few
reached these dizzy heights but none the less each trial was well patronized.

Ted carried on his hobby with me and we entered many trials together,
obtaining many varied certificates and trophies along the way in both Police and
Civilian Trials. We represented our Force a total of six times in Regional Trials
and also won through to the National Police Dog Championships held at
Preston, Lancashire. I did not win that, but as I was the only young lady to
qualify for that prestigious event I suppose you could say that, on that day, I was
the best police bitch in the country!

I think I enjoyed the civilian trials most because I met such a mixture of dogs
and I must have sniffed and played with most. Alsatians and Border Collies were
the most common but I have seen many different breeds competing, even a
Standard Poodle.

The only thing I did not like about either type of trial was the fact that both
sorts involved doing that horrid 'Sendaway' exercise so that meant that Ted
obviously wanted to train for it. He did his best to make a game of it and to get
me to like it, but I did not, and that was that. I cannot explain why. It did not
hurt. It was not a punishment. Occasionally, instead of running out to get me,
he would do a recall. In the end, on the run in I would leap into his arms instead
of sitting staidly in front of him like the book says. He later developed that trait
for demonstration and display purposes just to introduce a little more humour.
It seemed to amuse the crowds to see him carry me from the arena while I licked
his ear.

No matter how many dogs attended any one trial, I cannot recall having seen
one dog fight. Surely a tribute to both owners and dogs alike.

I did disgrace myself at one of the trials when I was a youngster. I was in the
back of the van while Ted was helping organise a local trial at Fort Bridgewood
in Rochester. One of the men acting the part of the 'criminal' got hurt and was
unable to continue so Ted was roped in to take his place. Well, the first time I
saw another dog chasing my 'Dad' across the field, I got so excited that I tore all
the wiring out of the back of the van. Ted was not amused when he saw it and
neither was the fitter who had to repair it at the workshops! Still, I only did it

once and I think that I redeemed myself over the years by earning him forty-eight certificates.

Are we next on?

Trials and Tribulations

I hope it won't rain
It's trials time again.
My husband won't sleep,
He'll keep counting sheep.
The days will go by
As he gives a sigh.
He says he's not ready
And Bess is not steady.
Later he's worse
Just shouts himself hoarse.
I'll try to be clever
And make an endeavour
To help all I can
With both dog and man.
The day's getting closer,
He's sure he's a loser.
How can I persuade him
To put on a brave grin?
But he's not on his own,
There's others who moan,
Their dogs all seem poorly,
Take Vetzymes four hourly!
All handlers get nervous,
It's worse than a circus.
They're training each day
With no extra pay.
Going out at all hours
In sunshine and showers.
It's 'seeking and tracking',
And, 'You do the searching'.
The day's getting near
There's no time for beer.
We really must hurry
And not stop to worry.
At last the day's come
With all training done.
The men gathered round
Soon make quite a sound
With Sergeants times three

And others to see.
Everyone's busy
All making me dizzy.
Oh. Now they have started
The best friends have parted
To go separate ways.
They've been waiting for days
To put their dogs through it,
And now that they do it
It's not nearly so bad
As some days they've had.
The dogs are so keen
To jump and retrieve
When commanded to speak
Some just make a squeak.
They 'seek' and they 'find',
Leaving handlers behind.
A 'Ten minute down',
Gives some handlers a frown
As some dogs will stay
And some be away!
But judges are human,
Talk freely to each man
About things they have done,
Points lost and points won.
And as they're progressing
Tight nerves start relaxing.
It's all like a game
With chances the same
The best dog will win,
His handler with him.
And now it's all done
Folk wend their way home.
'It's been a good day,'
They each stop to say.
Then I know that that's all
Till the next trials fall,
When we start once again
With 'I hope it won't rain.'

Jan

65

Stand Off or Not

Earlier on Bess referred to an exercise called 'The Stand Off'. A lot of handlers discuss the merits of it and whether it is worth all the effort involved in the training for it.

The principle is that should a criminal, after whom a dog has been sent, suddenly decide that discretion is the better part of valour and stop running, then the dog should not bite but should circle the man and bark, thus containing him until the handler arrives on the scene.

I know that as far as I am concerned it has been useful on more than one occasion.

One night I was on patrol and in crew was the night duty detective. We were having a look round an area for a man who had been seen tampering with motor vehicles.

The information came in too late for me to be of service, other than to be in the area in case he was sighted again.

I was lying down, head up but dozing as Ted drove slowly round, looking for any person answering the description.

The van stopped suddenly. I was up and alert, sensing that work might be imminent. Ted let the van roll back slowly as he turned the lights off. He then turned left sharply and accelerated hard as he switched the lights back on full.

As we sped into the car park I looked over his shoulder. All thoughts of sleep had gone. I could see a man in a white shirt at the door of the isolated car. As the lights shone on him he looked up and then ran across the car park towards the adjoining recreation ground on the far side.

The van bumped over the low pavement as Ted drove after him. I could see him clearly in the headlights as we gained very rapidly. Ted shouted through the open window. 'Stand still, Mate, or I'll release the dog.' The fleeing man could have had no doubts that there was a dog in the van because I was barking like mad in my excitement, but still he ran.

The man changed direction and I felt the van skid and lurch to a halt. Ted was at the rear doors of the van very quickly. 'Pas Auf' Ted shouted as he opened the doors for me. The detective, in the meantime, had got caught up in the excitement of the chase and was already after the fleeing man, having forgotten what I was there for. 'Stand still, Peter,' Ted yelled at the top of his voice. I skirted around the detective as he skidded to a halt, feeling a bit apprehensive and perhaps a little foolish too.

He need not have worried though, I only had eyes for the man in the white shirt who was running towards the railings which surrounded the recreation ground. I reached him at the same time as he dived for a hole in the ironwork. I grabbed for his elbow and then felt a terrific blow on the side of my head as I collided with the railings as he went through.

Ted got through the hole and grabbed the man, who was a gypsy from out of the area. He was handcuffed and marched back to the van to await another car

'The Chatham, Rochester & Gillingham News' printed this picture of us with their report that we had won a place at the National Police Dog Trials.

to take him away to the police station. Ted felt me all over and found a large bump and a small cut on my head. It would be sore for a while but not as sore as the gypsy's elbow, I'll bet.

Ted drove the van out of the recreation ground and back to the car where we had first seen the would-be thief. In the driver's door was the broken half of a key. The other half was on a key ring still in the possession of the gypsy.

The detective was very pleased that Ted still believed in training for the 'stand-off'. The gypsy was not.

Decorating

Because I was occasionally let indoors at home, some of Ted's workmates light-heartedly accused him of mollycoddling me. Although it was done in good humour, I felt sorry for their dogs if they were stuck in their compounds all the time that they were not at work.

One day one of these friends was bringing his wife over for a visit. Jan thought that it would be a good opportunity to really have a joke on him.

Ted had some royal blue carpet which he fitted in my kennel. He found all my trials certificates and trophies and decorated my kennel walls with them. Jan made some curtains out of some old nets that she had. To cap it all, she put a vase of flowers in one corner.

Net curtains and all!

It was a nice day and they all had tea out in the garden. During a lull in the conversation the visiting handler wandered down the garden to say hello to me in my compound. Well, you should have seen his face when he saw the curtains up at the window. He insisted that his wife should come and look and everyone had a good laugh as they saw all the trimmings.

Ted kept a straight face and said he thought that all handlers looked after their dogs in this way!

The Ghost of Bluebell Hill

It was the early hours during a particularly busy night shift. Once again the force radio burbled into life and we were making our way to Bluebell Hill. I obtained scant details from the Inspector at the scene and took Bess to where a car rug was spread out on the grass verge.

'Track on Bessie.'

I shook once to make the harness comfortable and started to work. There was scent at the car rug but it only led back towards the group of officers and ambulance men. Ted cast me round the other sides of it and slightly further away. I tried and I tried but nothing.

Ted praised me for my efforts and, after taking me out of harness, set me to work searching the hedgerows in the area.

Searching is second best only to tracking for me and I love it. I eagerly raced up and down the hedges where Ted directed me. I put flight to a terrified weasel. I smelled the rabbits that the weasel had probably been hunting. I just could not find the scent that I was looking for — human.

I dropped my van keys for Bess to find before she finished, as a 'sweetener'.

I completed the hedges and Ted allowed me to search on the grass verge for a while. Suddenly, I homed in onto human scent. The keys were buried deep in a tussock of grass but the slightest encouragement from Ted and I was on my way back to him with them jangling between my teeth. Ted went into his usual amount of praise and I was content knowing that he was pleased. I was back on my lead and sitting beside Ted while he fussed my ear.

We listened to a very strange tale from a motorist. He had been travelling up Bluebell Hill when a lady had stepped out in front of him. He had no time to take evasive action. The lady was struck so hard by the front of the car that she was thrown right over it, landing on the road. The driver stopped and went to the lady who was bleeding badly.

He took a car rug from his boot and gently put the injured woman onto it to move her to the grass verge and safety. The road was deserted at that time in the morning and he could not expect help from anyone. He left the lady on the rug and drove like fury to Rochester police station to report the accident and obtain help.

The emergency services arrived at the scene with the motorist. All that was there was the car rug, spread neatly out on the grass verge. There was no sign of the lady. There was no blood anywhere. The damage on his car had disappeared. Had I been trying to track the infamous Ghost Lady of Bluebell Hill?

Incentive

There were very many times when I ran tracks without finding anybody or any property. There were many reasons why. Sometimes the offenders had used a vehicle or the offence had been committed in a densely populated area and the track had been obliterated by passers by.

Without fail on occasions like these, Ted would make sure that he laid me a training track as soon as possible after the failure. When asked why he did this he would say that the reward at the end of a successful track was the incentive for me to work the next time. He called it 'a sweetener', and no matter how tired he was after a hectic night shift we always did one so that I could finish the shift on a good note and with plenty of praise.

'Rakes' in a Kentish Garden

Bluebell Hill, although it was not really on Ted's area, figured in my life yet again, not so long after.

Two white Jaguar cars had been seen speeding along the Rochester to Maidstone Road, late at night. A patrolling officer had carried out a check on the index numbers and one of the cars had been reported stolen. Some time later both Jaguars had been found apparently abandoned, in a small lane at the bottom of Bluebell Hill.

As we drove into the lane I could see that one of the Jaguars was minus a wheel and its boot and bonnet were open. It was in the process of being stripped for spares.

The local police motor cyclist who had found them, had not seen anyone when he arrived, so sat waiting quietly for us.

Into harness yet again. I never tire of it. The scent was fairly fresh and easy to follow. The motor cyclist had obviously disturbed the two offenders.

The track ran very erratically across the ploughed fields and along hedgerows. It was becoming obvious that these two were strangers to the area and were not sure where they were going.

Through a hedge. Across Bluebell Hill, watching out for traffic on the dual carriageway. Over a fence and up a bank. The scent was getting stronger now. We entered a private garden by going over the fence at the bottom. The track led up to a garden shed and the line rasped noisily against the woodwork as I rounded the corner.

I heard it rather than saw it. The implement whistled high above my head and crashed against the corner of the shed. He did not have time to swing the garden rake again because I had bitten him in the stomach.

The leather jacket must have taken most of the power of my bite, but still the man dropped the rake and shouted for Ted to call me off. The second man had heard his friend call out and stepped from behind the shed with his hands held high. Why do they do that?

Ted called me from the man I was holding and I left him, perhaps a little reluctantly, and went back to Ted. I watched the pair very carefully and they were left in no doubt as to what might happen if they tried anything else as silly as that. Even the chink of Ted's handcuffs did not distract me. He told the two men to come forward slowly. I barked very firmly and they both did exactly as they were told. They were very soon handcuffed together and were sitting on the ground having been searched.

We were able to relax a little now and Ted used his radio to direct a vehicle to us. I wandered behind the two men and I could not resist sticking my nose in the ear of one of them. I was only letting him know that I was still there but you should have seen them both jump!

The two men admitted that they had stolen the Jaguar car to strip it for spares and to syphon petrol out of it to get them back to Essex. They also said that they had not known that they were being followed by a police dog.

So that was why Ted was so slow in calling me out this time. He had realised that the rake had been aimed at him!

Egg and milk when I got home that morning confirmed that he was very pleased with me again.

Prince of Wales

There was much coming and going. The estate car was being loaded with cases and all manner of bits and pieces. I followed Ted backwards and forwards each time he went to the door. What on earth was going on? There was something up. It was only half past four in the morning and both Jan and Ted had had breakfast and I had already been out for a walk. What was going on?

I saw a bag of my dog biscuits being carried out, along with my food and water bowls. Now I was getting really worried. Were they going to take me? Was I included? Soon I had my answer. 'Come on girl.' I needed no second bidding and was at the back of the car like a shot. After the tailgate closed, I stood and watched, my breath steaming up the window, as Ted secured the house and put the last oddments in the car. We were off. Where to, I wondered?

We pulled out into the quiet streets. It reminded me of nights, but this was different. Jan was with us and we were in our own car, not the van.

Several hours and stops later we pulled up outside the old cottage in Llanrhidian, South Wales. Jan's cousin came out to greet us. It was the first time we had met but she had heard a lot about me from Jan's letters. She was very dog orientated because she had, quite coincidentally, married a South Wales police dog handler. Ted let me out of the car. It was good to stretch my legs again after such a long journey. The air was fresh and clean although tainted with the smell from the piggery just up the road. That did not worry me just then though, because Prince had been let out to meet me. His ears were erect, his tail arched, as he came towards me, the stranger on his territory. Our noses touched and his tail stuck up and wagged stiffly. He relaxed as he realised that I was not a threat to his domain. He was brown in colour and had a rather light coloured eye which gave him an unstable look. A look that had no doubt given the wrong-doers of the Swansea area something to think about.

The five barred gate which separated the garden from a large field was opened and we were allowed to run and get to know each other. I was enjoying the game very much when I realised that we were not the only animals in the field. It walked towards me and we touched noses. I felt and smelled the hot breath coming from its nostrils. The white saliva on its lips was tinged with green from the grass it had been chewing before we had so rudely interrupted it.

Jo and me with the 'Prince of Wales'

I had seen horses before. Ted had seen to that during my environmental training, but this one was different as I could look it straight in the eye! There were at least a dozen Shetland ponies in that field. I got on all right with them over the weekend but I would not trust them when they had their backs towards me and then gave them a wide berth. It was a lovely weekend and I thought that Wales was the best place I had ever been to. The cottage overlooked the Burry Estate and there were terrific views across the marshes and across the estuary itself. The sunsets were magnificent. The day after we arrived, Prince's handler packed some food for him and Ted and a bottle of water for Prince and me and we went for a walk. We walked all day! If we went out through the field where the Shetlands were we only had to cross one very minor marsh road all day. Not like Medway, I can tell you.

I was ready for my dinner that evening and, come bedtime, I snuggled down in the back of the estate car and dreamed until first light.

The following day Prince had to go to work, so Ted and I went out on our own. We went in the opposite direction this time and went up a huge hill called Cae Ifor tops. Ted took his binoculars with him and sat and watched the buzzards soar while I sniffed around fresh, interesting territory.

72

On the way back we came a different way and found ourselves walking along-side a wire fence. There were sheep on the other side and, although I had never been inclined to chase them before, Ted kept his eye on me. Funny things, sheep. They all scattered away from the fence as we walked along. Ted saw an unusual bird and stopped to watch it through his glasses. I sauntered along on my own for a few yards and I saw a 'sheep' which did not run away from the fence. I went to sniff it and touch noses in greeting through the wire, but it just backed away a few paces. I stood and looked at it for a second when it put its head down and charged at me. The fence bulged and I backed away. If it did not want to be friends, it only had to say. I had just met my first ram, and to be truthful, if they were all like that one, I did not mind if I never saw another. I was quite pleased to see that Ted gave that part of the fence a wide berth too! Us Townies!

A lovely weekend came to an end all too soon. We travelled back on the Tuesday and all agreed that we had needed that short break.

Paddock Punch-up

'Quiet tonight,' commented the night duty detective. Famous last words. Ted drove the van from Railway Terrace into the Paddock. The headlights picked out a large group of youths. They were gathered round two others who were fighting like fury. As Ted stopped with the van's headlights shining directly onto the group, they started to split up. One of the scrappers, realising that we were there, broke away and ran down the Paddock past the van. Ted challenged him to stand still as he rapidly got out of the driving seat. As the detective went forward to grab the other youth, Ted released me from the back of the van.

The youth was moving very fast down the Paddock and he turned right into Railway Terrace. I almost skidded round the corner.

There he was. His momentum had carried him across the road and he was now haring down past the Post Office.

The public house opposite had just turned out its late night revellers onto the street. They were scattered first by the youth, then by me and then by Ted. I rapidly caught up with the fleeing person but his arm was pumping backwards and forwards so fast that I could not get my timing right at that speed. So. I took the next best thing. His backside was not moving about quite so much so I took hold of that!

Again the now familiar salty taste as my teeth grazed his skin. He let out a scream and stopped running. I released my grip as Ted came up. As I let go, a large piece of material came with me. Ted called me to heel, took the youth by the arm and we all marched back to where the van had been left, again passing through the late night revellers, who were highly amused.

When I reached the van, the detective had, in the meantime, called for an ambulance for the other pugilist. His eye injuries were so bad that the ambulance went directly to Maidstone Eye Hospital.

Everything calmed down, Ted bent down to give me a pat and some praise and realised that I was still holding the piece of trouser material between my teeth. No wonder the crowds had been amused but I also wonder how many potential trouble makers were put off that night?

Finders Streakers

The headlights picked out the gleaming figures as they ran across Dock Road in front of us. I could see them clearly as they ran into the alleyway behind St Mary's Church. Ted pulled up at the end of the alley.

The two soldiers having had a good night out had decided to have a laugh on their way back to barracks. It was 1.30am and they were not really doing any harm. It was just their bad luck to decide to 'streak' in front of a police vehicle. Even worse bad luck that it was a police dog vehicle!

Ted took me out of the van and I am sure he was laughing. 'Go seek then,' he said, quietly and without the usual challenge.

I left him there in Dock Road and ran off into the comparative darkness. It was only a moment or two before I found the two men. Their giggles turned to gasps as they stood there, one arm clutching a bundle of clothing. I had never found a naked person before let alone two. They looked most odd standing there in the moonlight with their one spare hand clasped in front of them protecting what they thought were their most vulnerable parts. It was a fairly cold night and when I touched my healthy cold, wet nose against the backside of one of them, he leapt forward with a gasp. He probably thought that his end had come, as did his friend when I barked to let Ted know that I had found them.

He came along the pathway with the torchlight dancing in front of him. He laughed out loud when he saw the predicament of the two soldiers.

Ted put me on the lead and we escorted the two men back to the van. He put the pair of them into the spare cage, having placed their bundles onto the front passenger seat.

The two men were silent as I eyed them through the wire mesh which separated us.

The van pulled up outside the guardroom at Brompton Barracks and the orderly officer came out to meet Ted as he got out of the van.

'Hello, Sir. I've got two of your chaps here,' Ted said, as he tried to keep a straight face. 'Oh yes, and what have they been up to?' Ted opened the back doors of the van and the two hapless streakers clambered out.

The orderly officer and Ted stood beside the van and fairly rolled up as the two naked men were marched in double time back to their billet by a very stern guard commander. 'They were only having a bit of a giggle really,' Ted told the orderly officer. 'Yes. I think they've been punished enough, don't you?'

Jack. A New Recruit

The grey cement dust clung to my long fur. It was between my toes and covered the false floor of the van where I had been lying for nearly six hours, apart from two very quick excursions to answer the call of nature. I tried to clean up my feet but did not like the taste of it so it would have to wait until Ted groomed me.

We had been on a boring stint of observations at Northfleet. Ted reached over to the passenger seat and shook the long-emptied coffee flask.

The observations had proved a waste of time and it was approaching four o'clock in the morning as we were stood down. We were now free to make our way back home.

Ted stopped at Cobham Hall and I had a good run in the wet grass, while he wiped the dust from the back of the van as best he could. I felt better after that. Wet footed but certainly cleaner. 'O.K. Bess. Let's go and find a cup of tea and a seat that doesn't move, for ten minutes.'

We drove through Strood, on our way to Rochester police station. The day was just beginning for some early people on their way to work, ours was just about to end.

I was looking over Ted's shoulder as he negotiated the double bend under the railway bridge. There, ahead of us, was the local police area car. It was parked at an odd angle, outside a little old 'second hand' shop. Ted stopped as a police officer came out through the broken front door. 'Hello Ted. We've just come across this smash and grab. My crewman is having a look round the alleys at the back.' Ted cursed himself for not having changed back to the normal radio channel. He would have heard all this going on and we could have been there sooner. The second officer came back.

'I've had a good look round. I thought I heard something but it must have been a cat.' Ted said, 'You've got to wait for the keyholder anyway so I'll have a walk through the alleys with the bitch and see if we can flush anyone out.'

We had only just started to walk down the side road to the entrance to the alleyways, when there was a clatter ahead of us. A man came running out of the first alley and away down the road like a scalded cat. Ted challenged him but he did not stop. This was just like a training exercise. It just does not happen like this. The chain was off. The pads of my feet felt hot as I ran along the tarmac road surface.

I rapidly overhauled the man. He must have realised that I was almost upon him because he suddenly stopped, stock still, with his arms pointing skywards.

My speed took me past him and I missed him by a foot. I could not bite him but I could not resist giving one almighty growl as I skidded to a halt. All the fight went out of him as I stood there barking, until Ted and the other officers came running up.

The man was quickly handcuffed and, as we were walking back to the vehicles, Ted said 'Where's your mate?' 'You find him yourself,' replied the man, a little braver now that I was on a lead. At least we now knew that there were two of them. He was safely ensconced in the back of the police car. I sat beside Ted as he spoke to the other officers about the next plan of action. 'This area is very old and is riddled with alleyways.' My ears pricked up, well, as much as they ever could, my head on one side. Ted obviously saw the signs. 'Listen,' he said. All three men became quiet. Way in the distance a Jack Russell had started barking. I knew that he was not just barking to welcome the day. Something had disturbed him and he was protecting his domain, such was the urgency of his warning. 'I'll check that out first,' Ted told the other two. By walking down the side street, we were able to listen at the entrance to each alley and eventually identified the one where, in the distance, little Jack Russell was still doing his job. 'Seek on, Bess.' I fairly raced along the alley. Ted and one of the officers pounded along behind me. 'Keep going Jack. I'm nearly with you.' I approached the garden gate where the little dog was shouting his head off. There it was. In the garden next door. Human scent, very strong. The Jack Russell's nose was pointing under the fence in confirmation to where I knew the man was hiding.

I scratched at the ramshackle shed and joined the little Terrier in telling Ted where he was.

Ted shone his torch in the shed and there was the second man. He too, was handcuffed and when he was searched, some small silver trinkets were found in his pockets. Jack Russell snorted in defiance as the man was led away. The six hours of fruitless observations seemed ages ago. The remaining cement dust now seemed unimportant. I reckon little Jack Russell deserved a medal.

Food for Thought

At one time I used to buy dog food in bulk. There was an old lady along the road from us and we used to get together and buy food in such quantity that it was cheaper.

One day I found that a shop in Twydall Green had reduced its prices so I went to stock up.

I loaded up two supermarket trolleys and trundled them back to the estate car where Bess was dozing.

I livened up as the key went into the lock, and was ready to jump out. No. This was one of the occasions when I was actually encouraged to get over onto the back seat so that the cargo area was free for the enormous amount of 'Chappie'.

Ted was busy filling the load space from the creaking trolleys when a lady shopper walked by. She saw the vast number of trays of dog food and rather lamely, said 'Have you got a dog then?' Ted replied with a very straight face. 'No love, I run the café round the corner!' The lady walked away not knowing whether to smile or not. I cringed.

Peace and Goodwill to All Men

0220hrs. Christmas morning. We had been very busy. Mostly involving drunks who, by 'policemanship' had been sent on their way home, bearing in mind the time of year. The radio crackled into life yet again. 'Go to Conifer Drive re: "Burglary".' 'Wilco and a Merry Christmas to you, too.'

Ted was obviously feeling a bit fed up. We parked and had to walk some distance to the house in question. The owner was waiting outside. Because it was so far from the van, Ted took me on the lead and slung my tracking equipment over his shoulder, in case it was needed. I sniffed at it eagerly, anticipating work. I sat patiently beside Ted as the man started to relate his tale.

Suddenly, there was a commotion coming through the walkway from the next street. Again I perked up, expecting work. 'Excuse me, Mate, I'll just go and see what that's all about,' said Ted. Again. Famous last words!

We walked rapidly round the corner and saw a large number of men and a woman, hammering on the front door of a modern terraced house. Ted walked across the open plan gardens towards the group. 'Down Bess.'

I lay down as he walked the last few yards to get between the people and the front door of the house.

I was apprehensive and wriggled forward a bit, not wanting to disobey Ted, but also not wanting to be far away from him while he was with this ugly group.

The group were surprised to see him and were momentarily subdued and I thought things were going to be all right.

'O.K. Now. Tell me what the score is. What's the problem?' Ted grunted as a fist smashed against the side of his face. I leapt forward, my lead trailing, as he shouted my name. He grabbed the assailant with one hand and my lead with the other. All hell let loose. I felt a kick to my shoulder and turned in time to bite the calf above the foot which had caused my pain.

Instinctively, Ted put his back against a Transit pick-up which was parked in the driveway of the house. He had his assailant's long hair wound around his left hand. He was not going anywhere, despite the efforts of his drunken girlfriend, trying to release Ted's hand.

The rest of the group were trying to get at Ted and despite my efforts, got quite a few punches and kicks in.

There was one man who was extremely large, much bigger than Ted, whom I bit solidly in the stomach. He fell back and sat on the grass and cried! He was still there when reinforcements arrived, having been summoned by numerous '999' calls from neighbours who feared an outbreak of World War Three.

So had Ted. He was a sorry sight. He had been hit and kicked several times. Blood seeped from the corner of his mouth. His tunic was ripped and his flat police cap had been screwed up and trampled upon. His space beam torch? Well. That would never work again, it was in dozens of pieces.

I had been kicked a few times too, and I ached, but not as much as the five out of the seven whom I had bitten. Two of them had to go to hospital where I suspected that their treatment, by nurses who knew Ted, would be as unpleasant again!

The front door of the house, complete with its frame, was torn from the wall and now lay in the hallway. Every front window of the house was smashed. I am afraid the original caller who reported a burglary at his house did not get it sorted out that night, just because of what turned out to be a domestic dispute.

I was very pleased to overhear a conversation between another dog handler and Ted, a couple of days later, in which he said 'I would not have wanted any other dog with me that night, she was terrific.'

Court Jester — Caught Out

One of Ted's pranks almost backfired following a call to suspected intruders on premises at the Crown Court building after the alarm went off. It was a very large building to search and had to be done floor by floor. Ted and I first, followed by uniformed officers. We got to the final floor and it was becoming obvious that it was yet another false alarm.

We completed the search and Ted heard the lift coming up. He whispered, 'Down.' He ran off and returned very quickly wearing the wig and gown of a barrister. He even surprised me at first because I did not expect to see him dressed like that. As the lift came higher through the building, he stood very close to the lift door, with his thumbs in his lapels. He was going to make his colleagues jump as the doors opened.

The doors did open, and there stood the keyholder of the premises! I don't know who was more surprised but I do know that Ted went quite red and stayed that way for some time.

A good laugh was had by all, at Ted's expense.

Presents Retrieved Down Under

I heard the call and we started to make our way to St Williams Hospital, Rochester. We had not been asked for yet, but we were not engaged and I thought that we might be of some assistance.

A young Australian nurse was asleep in the nurses' quarters at the hospital. She had woken to find a man going through her belongings. She had shouted at him and he had darted through the open door and down the fire escape.

When we arrived, Ted cast me around the fire escape but the ground was so fouled up with the scent of the searching policemen that to track was impossible. If only they had waited a bit before stomping all over the place.

I tried all likely places but nothing. Ted stood with his back to the nurses' home. He surveyed the scene quietly. Where would he go if he had to get out of sight in a hurry?

Across the other side of St Williams Way was the entrance to a dark alleyway which led to the rear gardens of all the houses on that side of the road.

We walked over there. 'Track on, Bessie.' It was good to find a scent to follow, after all the effort earlier with nothing to show for it.

Yes. It was definitely there. Ted came with me, holding the line fairly short, as I started to track into the blackness.

The radio came to life. It would appear that someone had been seen running in City Way, which was right across the other side of the hospital, and totally in the opposite direction to where we were going. Lots of radios crackled into life as officers responded and started to rush to that area. I thought that there were enough of them to sort that out. Bess was tracking and I trusted her and would follow this track to its conclusion no matter what.

Along dark and smelly alleys the scent led. Twisting and turning and crossing roads. This man knew every short cut which would keep him off open and exposed roads for as long as possible.

The hullabaloo on the radio seemed to die down and the sighting in City Way was resolved. Ted found time and air space to tell the radio controller what we were doing.

We were tracking along alleyways parallel with St Williams Way. A sergeant in a car kept pace with us but stayed on that road so that he did not interfere with the scent that I was following.

Quite soon, I found myself out of the alleys and into the closed off end of a cul-de-sac. The track was more difficult now as it was all hard surface. It was getting quite old in time too, because of all the delay at the hospital. I was picking my way along the pavement when I suddenly realised that the scent was no longer there, in front of me. Ted recognised the signs and stood perfectly still. Quiet words of encouragement reached me and intensified my efforts.

Casting to the right, I found the tell tale scent on the lowest step of a flight of six. Up to the front door I went. 'Well Ted. Now it's up to you. I've done my bit.'

The house was in darkness. Ted pulled me back. 'Good girl. Come on.' He coiled up the tracking line as we walked back into the shadows of the alley. He took off my harness and replaced it with chain and lead. He used the radio and asked if any officer on watch had any knowledge of the occupants of the house where the track had terminated.

Within minutes, a torch flashed in the alley behind us and we were joined by the night duty detective for that area.

'I know the man at that address and this job is just up his street.' We, all three, went and knocked at the door. It was eventually answered by a lady who had obviously been awakened from her slumbers. 'Hello, love, sorry to disturb you, but is John in?' the detective asked.

'He's in bed asleep,' she said as she rubbed her eyes. 'We'd like to check that, please.'

'Come in, but be quiet,' said the lady. I quite liked her. She told the detective where her son slept and we all went upstairs. The officer opened the door and switched on the light. I could see a man in bed with the bedclothes pulled up high around his neck. He looked to me as if he was asleep. Ted walked forward. He had seen the strap just sticking out from under the bed. He pulled out a camera. The D.C. said 'Come on, John. We know you're awake.' He reached forward and tugged on the bedding. The man was fully dressed!

He got up and was handcuffed. Ted got down on his knees and from under the bed removed a watch and some jewellery which had been hurriedly secreted under there. I felt sorry for his mother who was standing in the doorway, sobbing.

A car took the prisoner away and the D.C. and Ted, with me very comfortable on the back seat of a fairly new C.I.D. car, took the stolen property back to the hospital. The young Australian nurse was ecstatic. She was due to fly home in two days' time and she thought that she had lost all the presents bought for her family.

I got a great deal of fuss from a pretty suntanned young lady who was still dressed in her nightie. No wonder the police had stayed so long!

Blood Donor Bess

'Come on Bess. You can help out here.' Ted took me out of the van and into the surgery on the lead. He had popped in to the vet's on a social visit.

Whilst we were there a labrador dog was brought in, having been involved in an accident. He was in a very bad way apparently although I did not see him. 'Feet up, Bess.'

I was used to this by now and stood with my feet up on the edge of the operating table. Ted lifted me until I was able to sit and survey the room. You get a completely different outlook from up here, you know.

The vet came through with a nurse. The electric razor began to hum and he came towards me. 'Hey. What's that you're doing. There's nothing wrong with me!'

'Good girl, Bess,' he said as he promptly shaved a great lump of hair from my neck. What was going on? I now had a great bald patch. Another nurse came in and the vet went away with her. Ted followed them. 'Stay. Bess.'

I felt odd, sitting up there all alone. I sniffed at the great wad of hair on the table in front of me but it did not jump back into its rightful place.

A minute later Ted was back with the vet. 'Oh. Well. It was worth a try but he was too far gone.' Apparently I was going to give that labrador some of my blood but sadly he had died before I could help. It seems that any dog can give blood to any other dog, not like you people, who have to be kept in groups.

Gang Warfare

One of my favourite places for going for a walk when we were off duty was the local recreation ground. Ted took me to private land down by the River Medway for a run and then we walked on the roads to keep my nails down and ended up in the rec for a game. There were many people there who knew me and stopped to chat with Ted while they made a fuss of me.

We went in there one day to find that the children had tied a rope up in a tree and had put an old tyre at the bottom to make a swing. As we passed it Ted gave it a nudge. As it swung back I grabbed it and had a right old game, to the amusement of onlookers. 'Well I AM off duty you know.'

Another evening we were in the same rec off duty, when it became necessary for me to go on duty. We were just having our last stroll of the day. It was late and quite dark. There suddenly came a hullabaloo as a large gang of youths entered the rec at the far end. There was no doubt that they were looking for trouble. They were chanting about looking for a rival gang and they all had sticks and pieces of fence posts.

I could feel the tension in the air. The lead tightened as Ted adjusted his grip while he walked towards them. Ted stopped in front of them and told them to put the sticks down while he spoke to them. Some of the youths knew Ted and me, and dropped their weapons straight away. 'Right. Now see sense. Go home and cool off.'

I barked. More sticks fell to the ground and I heard 'Police' muttered as the word went round the group from those who knew us. There were just five left who did not put their weapons down. Ted spoke again to them but a punk type, who was obviously the ringleader, came forward with his stick raised. The lead slackened and I went forward. 'Pas Auf.'

My teeth scored his thigh as I bit through his trousers. The youth fell back against his friends, whose courage was rapidly diminishing. Whether it was bravado or just plain stupidity, he came forward again. I bit higher and harder this time, catching the youth in the stomach. He screamed and dropped the stick. 'Leave, Bess.'

I did so, if a little reluctantly. The man's courage failed him completely as he saw the last of his friends disappearing through a hole in the fence. He, too, followed them, holding first his thigh and then his stomach.

Ted gathered up the sticks and other weapons and we made our way to the police station. He was fed up. He did not want to get involved in this sort of thing when he was off duty but neither could he stand by and watch it go on. At the station I lay in the corner while he made a full entry in the occurrence book.

The station officer told Ted that they had received three calls about that gang during the evening! They did not get any more!

In the Swim

Night duty and Ted had parked in his usual spot by the Town Hall. He could see right along Military Road from here and there were quite a few people around.

One of his taxi driver acquaintances pulled up alongside the van. The driver leant over and lowered his nearside window to talk to Ted without getting out of his taxi.

'I've just made a drop over at Rochester and I came past the swimming pool. There were a couple of herberts hanging round the front door. The place has been closed for ages.' Ted thanked him and with one last look along Military Road to make sure that it was still quiet, we made our way towards Rochester. He stopped the van some way away from the swimming pool and put me into my leather night collar. We walked quietly in the shadows towards the front of the building to make sure that it was secure anyway. He flashed his torch briefly onto the lower part of the wooden front door. The lower section of it was missing where heavy boots had made short work of it. 'Quiet girl.' 'Don't worry Ted, I wasn't going to say anything.' Ted was down by the hole, listening. I growled. I could hear somebody moving around in there.

Ted crawled quietly through the opening. Well, as quiet as he could, anyway. I followed him and we stood in the darkness letting our eyes become accustomed to the gloom as soon as possible.

We could hear voices now. Low and echoey in the cavernous building. Ted stepped into the main area and switched his torch on.

'Police officer with a dog. Come out now or I'll send the dog in.'

The torchlight picked out two skinhead types in the process of opening the office door with a large screwdriver. They shielded their eyes, trying to look beyond the beam. I thought that they needed a little more convincing as to who had caught them in the act, so I barked. The sound almost caught me by surprise it was so loud, but I liked it and did it again.

The yellow-handled screw driver fell to the ground as both of them put their hands in the air. I think that they had been watching too many cowboy movies.

I used my radio and summoned another police car to take the two men away. They had done quite a lot of damage but had not gained access to the office containing the safe. I waited until the keyholder had arrived and made the place secure before I went to get on with the necessary paperwork.

By the time we resumed patrol the streets were fairly quiet and I had time to try to find the taxi driver in order to let him know the result of his information and to thank him.

I found him outside the railway station where he was getting a hard time from three youths who were arguing about the fare on his taxi meter.

Ted got me out of the van and we just stood beside our vehicle looking directly at the taxi and the three youths. Their noise subsided quite quickly and they left the taxi driver and moved away into the railway station having paid their fare.

Well. One good turn deserves another, eh?

Hide and Slide

I heard the footsteps long before Ted did. I tried my hardest to prick up my ears. He turned and saw the officer strolling across the car park.

It was an unusually quiet night. Ted, on more than one occasion, had checked the radio to make sure that it was still working.

At two thirty that morning Ted had rolled the van to a halt in the car park at Gillingham Strand. He leaned against the front of the vehicle, taking the night air whilst listening in vain, in case the radio came to life. I was stretching my legs and sniffing the grass which surrounded the car park. 'Hello Mate,' Ted greeted him. I wandered over to meet the foot patrol officer. 'Hello, Bess. How are you tonight?' The two men stood talking for a while. 'Do you want me to hide up for her, Ted?'

It was an offer that not many non-dog handling officers would make so Ted accepted, pleased for something to do. 'Just go out there and hide anywhere you like. Don't move when she finds you.'

Ted put me back into the van and we drove off to return some ten minutes later. 'Hey you out there. Come out or I'll send the dog in to find you,' he shouted. The only reply was from me as I bounced at the end of the lead. 'This is your last chance. Come out now.' Ted had trouble removing my check chain because I was so keen to get working. 'Go seek, Bess.' I darted off into the darkness. Checked the public toilets, inside and out. Nothing there. Checked the outside of the swimming pool running at full tilt. My nails made grooves in the grass as I skidded to a halt. If I lifted my head and tested the air, I could detect human scent. 'Yes. That's definitely it, and it's coming from up high.'

Breaking into a run again, I followed the scent as it wafted towards me from the children's playground. In the darkness I almost bumped into the bottom of the children's slide.

The scent was tumbling down the ironwork, forming invisible pools on the ground before being carried away by the breeze. I went to the steps at the other end of the apparatus. First one foot, then another as I made my way up the wrought iron ladder.

As I clambered I heard a movement from the little cage at the top, as the man moved uncomfortably. He knew that I was climbing towards him.' 'There he is.' He had made himself as small as possible and had squeezed into an area designed to take two small children at the most. 'Well. If he can get in there, so can I!'

I ended up standing virtually across his drawn up knees. My head was inches from his hands which were clasped tightly over his face. As per my training, I now had to let Ted know that I had found him and exactly where he was, so I barked.

With each bark the man jumped, expecting to be bitten at any moment. 'T-e-d,' he called out, very tentatively. I barked. 'T-e-d.' I barked again. Ted shone his torch up the slide and just could not help laughing when he saw that the little cage was full of man and dog. 'Bessie. Leave. Come on.' With my nails extended to slow me slightly, I slid down the highly polished surface to where Ted was waiting with my praise. The apparatus vibrated as the officer clambered back down the steps. 'You rotten so-and-so. You didn't tell me that she could climb as well!' he said, good humouredly.

'You didn't ask,' said Ted, and went on to explain how I use the slide in our local recreation ground to entertain the local kids.

Broadmoor Bound

'Operations here. Could you turn out to Strood.' Ted put the phone down. I needed no second bidding as he opened the back gate, and I was waiting at the van door long before he got there. I instinctively knew that we were going to work even though Ted was not in uniform. The blue light was whirring above my head. Occasionally, the two tone horns blared out, warning traffic of our approach at speed. I stood up, leaning into the bends, as Ted weaved through the evening traffic.

We arrived to find a traffic motor cyclist who told me this story. He was on patrol in Strood when he heard a Volkswagen Beetle car with a noisy exhaust system and wanted to speak to the driver about it. A chase had ensued around the back streets of the town. Householders were at their doors, waiting for the Volkswagen and the motor cycle to come round again, such was the commotion.

The car was eventually driven into a public footpath until it got wedged where the path narrowed. The driver had climbed out through the sun roof and had run off down the alley. The wedged car blocked any chance of further pursuit.

The motor cyclist continued his story. 'It was a bit hairy. Every time I got alongside him, he waved a sickle at me out of the window. That is still in the car. He must be mental, the way he was driving.'

It must have looked quite funny to see Ted and me clambering over the Volkswagen Beetle with its sloping roof and bonnet, but we managed. On with the tracking harness and I found the scent very easily. In fact it could only go one way. The only problem was that I had just started when along came a group of people out for an evening stroll, their footsteps obliterating any scent of the offending driver. Ted spoke to them but they had seen nothing. I sniffed at their Jack Russell. Ted told them that the alleyway was blocked ahead of them and waited until they retreated back along the way they had come. The Jack Russell looked over his shoulder until they had all turned the corner. Ted had, by this time, taken me out of harness and the equipment was coiled neatly over his shoulder. Now that the pathway was clear, we started a search as we made our way along it. I was checking the thorny hedges on either side, while Ted called me back to check any opening where a person might have squeezed through. I had already checked them to my satisfaction but obviously not to his!

The path led out into wasteground which was a haven for people to walk their dogs on. Several came up to me for a friendly sniff. 'Can't they see that I'm working?'

The last dog left me and I was able to concentrate again. 'What's that? Yes. There it is.' A pool of scent where someone had squeezed through the hedge and under the barbed wire fence. I was through the hole when Ted said, 'Down. Bess.'

I waited impatiently while Ted got his considerable bulk through the hole and under the wire. Horrible stuff. 'Seek on girl. Where is he?' He need not really have said that. I was off. We were in a derelict orchard and it was easy to pick up the man's odour. I bounded forward, head up, not needing to track because I knew that he was ahead of us. The middle aged man stood up from the clump of nettles that had been hiding him from view. He looked as though he could not hurt a fly. I barked at him, as per my training, and he stood perfectly still, his hands by his sides. Ted searched him thoroughly and handcuffed him in view of the incident with the sickle. He also searched the nettles where the man had been hiding, but nothing. Getting the man back through the barbed wire was a palaver but we managed it by me going through first and waiting until the prisoner wriggled through, followed by Ted.

By the time we got back to the footpath, the car had been removed. The motor cyclist had gone too, patrolling the streets, looking for the man. I called up on the radio for transport for the prisoner and within minutes he was on his way to Rochester police station. The following day I had to go to the C.I.D. office at the station to make my statement regarding the previous evening's episode.

As usual when he was not going to be long, Ted took me in with him to see the typists and to wait in the corner whilst he did his writing. As we entered the office on this occasion the Detective Inspector was there. 'Hello, Ted. Nice job last night.'

'Thanks, Guv. Blimey, what have you got there?' The D.I. was holding a sawn-off shotgun in his hands. 'Look at the workmanship on this. It's only eleven inches long overall, and these.' He indicated the broad window sill beside him. 'These are .410 shotguns but he has made them like pistols. They are four and a half inches long.'

'Oh. Where'd they come from?' said Ted. 'That bloke you nicked last night. He owned the orchard where you found him. These were in the shed in the corner. Loaded, too.' Ted sat down with a gasp. 'Christ! Two minutes later and he would have had his hands on them.' We are both glad to say that the man is still in Broadmoor.

Wheel in the Evidence

'I don't know if you can help us or not, Ted.'

I sat beside him as Ted listened to the story from the officer who had put out the call for us. Two other officers stood beside an old car, watching the occupants carefully. The three policemen had attended an alarm to a school on the edge of the town. As they arrived the old car had started to drive out of the woods adjoining the school grounds and the officers had stopped it and detained the persons in it. One officer had then gone to check round the school and had found that a burglary had been committed.

There was nothing in the old car to connect the three men with the burglary. It was obvious that they were involved but there seemed to be little in the way of evidence.

Ted took me to where the officer had indicated the point of entry. Glass lay all around from where the door had been kicked in.

I was soon tracking away across the school playing field, meandering from scent to scent. Ted would know from my actions that we were following more than one person. Right in the middle of the field I lay down as the scent from an object filled my nostrils. Ted came along the slackened line. His torch picked out a length of plastic covered cable with a plug at either end. He picked it up and put it into his pocket. 'Track on girl. Let's see if you can find the rest of the television.'

The track took us through a hole in the boundary fence and into a building site. Through the site the track continued and out into the woods. The scent was now different somehow but I could not tell why.

I tracked on and out into a narrow muddy lane. We were both surprised to see the old car and the police officers a few yards along.

Ted put me into the down position and took off my harness. I was ready for play now having worked but, no, he kept me under control while he spoke quietly to one of the officers. I saw him take the cable from his pocket to show him. 'It's got to be around here somewhere. Hang on to those three while I search the woods.'

The low twigs and branches scratched at my face as I raced off into the darkness. I really do love searching and I only needed the slightest bidding from Ted.

The wind was coming through the woods so he directed me along the track for a while. Suddenly, I ran right into the dissipating plume of human scent as it was borne on the wind through the unkempt hedgerow. I squeezed through and I had no trouble wending my way along that ever narrowing invisible path of scent to its source. There it was: a builder's wheelbarrow and inside it a television and a projector. What to do now? Another sniff at it and it triggered my reflexes. I barked several times and then listened for Ted's encouragement. 'Good girl. Where is it then?'

I barked continuously as I watched his torch come bobbing through the trees towards me. He was followed by one of the officers. 'Oh. Brilliant,' he said as Ted's torch illuminated the wheelbarrow and its contents.

I stood by, on a taut lead, as the three men were told that they were being arrested and were placed into separate police cars. None of them put up a struggle and I do believe that they knew that the game was up.

When the last of the police cars had driven away, Ted threw my chain off into the darkness for my reward. He made so much fuss of me when I returned for him to do it again. The effort spent on training for the 'irretrievable article' had well and truly paid off.

Whatever Next

I had been feeling low for a couple of days. It was nothing that I could put my paw on, just a feeling of tiredness. I had also lost a few pounds in weight. That in itself was unusual because I always work at around ninety pounds. Ted was being particularly watchful. He had learned by experience and books, the basics of first aid for me and also how to watch out for the early signs of simple ailments. I had been to the toilet out in the rough ground of Motney Hill. Ted walked across to see what I had done. He does that quite frequently because a lot can be learned from the condition of my faeces. (He often moans because I usually go so far out of the way to do it too.) I looked on as he examined them to find traces of blood and mucus.

We went home and found a suitable container in which to collect a sample and later that day I found myself at the vet's in Gillingham again. Funnily enough, I never mind going there nowadays. Ted was very fortunate in having such a good vet so close to home. It was not unusual for Ted to sit in on operations when he had the time.

The vet examined the container. 'I think it will be Colitis, Ted, but I'll get this checked first.'

It was indeed an infection of the colon and my diet was changed straight away. You'll never guess what I have to eat now. All-Bran and Chappie! Yes, that's right. I always thought that so much fibre would not be good for you but given in the right quantities, it can be a bulk builder too. I was also put on a very expensive drug called Salazapyrin. (The police would not like paying for that, I knew.)

Although I would have to have this diet and treatment for the rest of my days, within two weeks I was back to health, feeling good and had regained my lost pounds.

It was lucky for me that Ted knows me so well, realised something was wrong and that the Colitis was discovered and treated early.

'It's a Fair Cop'

The stolen vehicle had crashed into a wall in St Margaret's Street, Rochester. The local police patrol car was already on the scene when we got there.

The tracking harness appeared as Ted released me from the back of the van. My front feet left the ground as I bounced with excitement at the thought of work. I love tracking.

The line burned Ted's fingers as he paid it out. Through the alley and out onto the grass banks, past the printing works. The track was strong. 'We are going towards the Esplanade and the river, if you can get someone to that area,' Ted puffed into the radio. We went right over the grass banks, through the recreation ground, and down towards the River Medway.

Looking ahead, I could see the lights of a police car which was parked at the side of the Esplanade. I pulled towards it in a straight line. Ted was really laying

.K
FBB FBC AND FBX
ROUTINE 210444AUG
FROM ROCHESTER
TO ALL SUBS B DIVN

                        ARREST MESSAGE

(1) ████████████████   ████████████ROCHESTER
(2) 0145 HRS 21 8 78 THE ESPLANADE ROCHESTER
(3) TAKING A CONVEYANCE
(4) FOLLOWING A COMPLAINT OF A CAR BEING STOLEN FROM KING
    EDWARD ROAD ROCHESTER THE VEHICLE WAS FOUND IN CHURCHFIELDS
    TERRACE BY PCS WADE AND DUNCAN T DIVN   PC WRIGHT ATTENDED
    WITH 'BESS' AND FOLLOWED A TRACK THROUGH A RECREATION GROUND
    TOWARDS THE ESPLANADE PASSING THIS INFORMATION TO PATROLS.
    SGT CHERRY AND PC LAMBOURNE WENT TO THE ESPLANADE WHERE
    THEY SAW ████ COME FROM THE RECREATION GROUND TO THE ROAD
    WHERE HE WAS STOPPED.   BESS MEANWHILE CONTINUED TO TRACK
    AND TOOK HER HANDLER TO THE SPOT WHERE ████ WAS DETAINED
    ████ LATER ADMITTED THE OFFENCE AND IS DETAINED AT ROCHESTER

AUTH PS CHERRY   SENDER PS CHERRY

back on my tracking line, obviously thinking that the officers had walked up the bank and I was now following their scent.

When we were about twenty yards from the vehicle I could see two uniformed officers standing beside it with a man who was not in uniform. I tracked right up to the three men, having to drag Ted as he was not sure.

'Stopped this guy coming off the banks after your message, Ted,' one of the officers said. The third man said 'O.K. It's a fair cop. It was me.'

Ted laughed out loud at the classic saying that he had never heard before, other than on television.

He was even happier when he later learned that the man had admitted two burglaries and other stolen vehicles.

Switching On

I was enjoying the attention. Hands fussing both my ears as I sat on the lounge carpet, directly in front of Ted's sister-in-law. She was staying for a while and I had been allowed in to be introduced to her. My eyes closed as she sat on the floor, legs crossed and directly in front of me, making a fuss of me.

Suddenly, over her shoulder, I saw Ted with his fist raised. 'No. That's can't be right. That's the signal for me to speak. There it is again. He does want me to bark. O.K. Here goes.' The lady virtually hopped across the floor on her backside until she was about six feet from me. Ted rolled up. Tears streamed down his face.

His sister-in-law also realised what had happened and she too, laughed. 'God. I thought she'd turned into a police dog.' Ted's sense of humour again!

Cold Comfort

The noise was deafening. Lights were coming on in the few occupied flats above the shops in nearby Station Road.

The alarm had only just started as Ted rolled the van slowly along the back streets around the shopping precinct, on what had been before that, a rather quiet and boring night.

We had only left the shopping precinct an hour earlier, at 2am, when I had laid Bess a short training track. Both for the training and for something to do.

The Co-op at Rainham was a comparatively new building and, like so many of its day, was constructed with a lot of glass panels. The precinct was quite well lighted but the covered walkways cast shadows causing parts of the outside of the building to be fairly dimly lit. It was difficult to check each pane of glass quickly without using a torch.

I sensed that this was different. The leather night collar was tighter than usual as Ted gripped the lead while he tested the glass panels which formed the wall of the check out area of the vast building. Everything seemed secure. The double reinforced glass doors rattled as Ted pushed and pulled them before we moved on.

He slipped my collar off and I trotted on ahead of him. 'Here Ted. Is this what you're looking for?'

I rounded the next corner to see the rear half of Bess as she stood looking into the store where the two foot square window had been neatly removed. I could tell from her attitude that she wanted to go into the building. As quietly as I could, I called her to me. She reluctantly put her head back into the leather collar. 'Just wait a minute, girl, you'll be working soon enough.'

We stood quietly as the approaching sound of other vehicles got louder. Ted spoke into his radio, directing the officers where to go to cut off any possible escape routes. The car engines stopped and a few doors banged and then only the urgent sound of the alarm was to be heard.

My eyes were still glued to that dark hole where the glass should have been. My head stretched forward as I tested the air. I knew that someone had crawled through that hole recently and I wanted to get to work.

Ted spoke into his radio again to let the policemen know that things were about to happen.

No need for quiet now. He challenged the building as he crouched down at the hole.

'Come on out mate. I know you're in there.' I too, let forth my own form of challenge by barking at the top of my voice. I thought I heard movement from deep within the building.

'Come on out. It's your last chance before the dog comes in.' The alarm was still going but whoever was in that store must have heard him.

'Go on Bess. Go seek.' The leather collar was whipped off over my head and I was away. I heard Ted crawling through the hole, his space beam torch jiggling about as he tried to check my progress.

Odd lights were on in the shop and these helped us both. I fairly charged up and down the aisles, through smells which at any other time could have been quite interesting. Smells of dog biscuits and other foods. All very tempting but not what I was there for. Something else took precedence over all others. I knew that there was someone in there and I wanted to find them. Up and down the aisles. Past stacks of washing powder and cleaning agents, past tins of beans and peas. The human scent was everywhere. My feet slid on the polished floor as I tried to stop. I was in the frozen food section. The scent was stronger and concentrated. Was that a noise I heard above the humming of the electric motors of the freezers? I sniffed intensely along the closed lid of one of the long white cabinets. Yes. Someone was near and was that movement I heard?

A bark was drawn from me almost automatically. Great encouragement from Ted in the distance brought more. I jumped up onto the top of the cabinet and felt the lid give way slightly under my weight. Ted came up with his torch on. I barked and barked with my head down.

'What have you got, girl?'

I scratched at the top of the freezer beneath my feet. My bark sounded strange because I was barking downwards.

'O.K. Bess. Off you get. Let's have a look.' I jumped down as he clicked his fingers but I could not resist sniffing along the seal of the lid. Ted moved along to the large handle and slowly lifted the lid. Vapour wafted out into the torch beam. As soon as the lid was opened far enough I stood with my front feet up on the edge. This time my bark came out properly as I saw the man inside. He was lying on top of frozen chickens and could not have been very comfortable.

'Come on out mate. There's nowhere for you to go.' Wonder why Ted always calls them 'Mate'?

The man stood up on his unstable 'perch' and carefully clambered over the side of the freezer cabinet. I barked at him again to let him know that I was still there. He stood quietly blowing on his finger-tips.

'What on earth made you hide in there?' Ted queried, 'You could have died.'

'It was the first place handy when I heard you shout. I couldn't hear the dog because of the motor so I opened the lid to have a look.'

He accepted the handcuffs without any trouble and we made our way to where the other officers were waiting at the hole. One of them pointed to the shrubbery on the other side of the path. 'The missing window is over there. Frame and all.'

Back at the police station Ted took me in with him and I lay quietly in the corner as he documented the man. I had no animosity towards the prisoner. In fact he looked rather pathetic. He looked towards me. 'Good dog you've got there, sir. What breed is it?'

Ted's eyes rolled up towards the ceiling as he smiled.

It Just Fell, Honest

Jan and Ted would take me virtually everywhere in the estate car when we were off duty. I hated the police kennels at Stockbury and Ted did not like me being there either.

I mentioned to a colleague that Jan and I had to go away for a while and that we could not take Bess with us. I was glad to say that the friend offered to have her at his home.

I knew the family very well and got on famously with the dogs that they owned. We all went for long walks, and played a lot. In fact it must have looked like a pack coming down the road whenever we were taken out.

I enjoyed myself there. It was not the same as being at home with Jan and Ted but they looked after me very well. In fact I became quite crafty. The lady was a pushover for an appealing look and I very soon found out that when I sat and looked up at a certain round thing which was always up there on the work surface, her hand would delve into it and re-appear with a nice biscuit!

I, once again, disgraced myself while I was there. The lady was defrosting her refrigerator and she emptied it and left the door wide open. I was just having a nose round really. All the dogs had finished playing outside and the patio door was open. I found myself in the kitchen and the sound of ice melting and falling in the fridge attracted me over to it. Well, I was just watching the ice melt when this half pound packet of butter fell off one of the door shelves and landed on the floor in front of me. I did not touch it, honest. At least I did not touch it until it was on the floor but then it was fair game, wasn't it?

Anyway, the inevitable happened and I was caught just finishing it off, paper and all. I half expected a good telling off but no, the lady just rushed away to use the telephone.

The vet laughed when she explained what had happened. He told her not to worry but in view of my Colitis problems, she should stand well clear when next she took me out to the waste ground. Cheek!

Deadly Call Out

I heard the chink of the check chain as the compound gate opened. I was having a nap before we started night duty at ten o'clock. This was yet another call out. Into the van and we were speeding towards the village of Hoo, just outside Rochester.

First of all, we went to the Hoo police office and collected the local Sergeant.

'Strange one this, Ted,' he said as he directed us through the country lanes. 'A man told his wife that he was popping out to the garage to get a screwdriver to repair some electrical implement in the house. He didn't come back in. She waited about two hours before she called us.' We pulled up outside a row of isolated farm cottages. The sergeant went into the house, leaving us to get on with our work.

91

Ted did not know where to start. It was a case of trial and error to begin with. He put me into harness near the garage door. The line paid out as I, with nose to the ground, made my way slowly down the garden.

'Track on girl,' softly came the words of encouragement. They were not really necessary as the appearance of the tracking equipment was all the incentive I needed. It was nice to know that he was there, though.

The garden was a mess. Long matted grass, overgrown with brambles and old apple trees. The odd piece of rusty metal waited to cut me if I trod on it wrongly. Yet among all this was the faint smell of a person and something else. Something evil and pungent to my keen senses.

I followed the scent slowly. It was not easy. The track was getting very old and I had to pick out every footprint. Two hundred and ten million hair sensors in my olfactory system worked overtime. I was under no pressure from Ted who knew that I was doing my best.

Along the overgrown path. Overhanging grass trodden down by a man's heavy tread. The odd squashed insect. The faint smell of leather and boot polish. All signs that I was travelling the right way. Even that awful smell was becoming of assistance to me.

Gradually we picked our way down the garden. Suddenly that pungent chemical was nearby and mixed with a concentration of human scent. There in the long grass beneath the branches of an apple tree which reached the ground, was a newspaper-wrapped bundle. Reflexes came into action and I lay down and waited for Ted to come forward.

'Good grief, Bess. What on earth have you found?' He carefully picked up the bundle and gently unwrapped it. It was a bottle and he read aloud from the stained label. 'Metasystox.' He placed the bottle back on the ground and walked me on a little way from it. Now that I was up wind of the bottle I could concentrate on the human scent in front of me.

Over the broken fence we went, Ted pausing long enough to confirm that someone else had passed this way before us. The sound of a vehicle and he hauled back on the line, waiting for the country lane to clear.

'Track on, Bessie. Good girl.' He gave me extra line to work with and I crossed the narrow lane. Yes. It was here all right. The scent and the visual signs that someone had climbed the bank. There was resistance on the line as Ted clambered up and we were off into the orchard.

I was puzzled. Ted had left that smelly bottle where I had found it with a view to collecting it later. Yet I was sure that awful smell was getting stronger again!

On through the trees, my speed increased as the scent was held longer on the virgin grass. Ted had to fend off low branches with a raised arm.

I was tracking so fast that I almost did not see him. He was crumpled up in long grass at the bottom of an apple tree. I lay down beside the dead man. The stench of the chemical was unbearable. The man's lips and cheeks were burned by toxic fluid.

Ted took me upwind of the man so that I was out of the chemical. He summoned the sergeant on the radio and he was on the scene quite soon. He was a man of considerable experience but even he was taken aback by the sight of the man's face.

I was glad when Ted was free to take me back to the van. He gave me a drink of fresh water and gently washed off my muzzle and paws in case I had come into contact with the noxious fluid. I had done my bit and now it was up to him and the other officers to get the paperwork sorted out.

I just cannot understand some of the things you people do.

The Bare Facts

I was bored. It was day duty and getting towards late afternoon. The radio was quiet and we had completed our training sessions for the day.

I decided that a little foot patrol in Chatham High Street might not go amiss.

He parked the van in one of the side roads and we walked into the High Street. I suppose it is not a very common sight for members of the public to see a policeman and his dog on foot patrol, even though we did it quite frequently in different parts of the Medway Towns. People tend to want to talk for some reason but that is what we are here for. I do not mind for I get lots of fuss and attention while they are talking to Ted. It is surprising really how many people say that they have a dog just like me at home but theirs is always bigger and blacker! They also think that because I have a long coat I am a German Shepherd dog instead of an Alsatian. Ted always has a chuckle to himself over that one.

Eventually we reached a part of the High Street where the shops were being refitted. Outside a ladies wear shop there was a builder's skip. Protruding from the skip, in a rather grotesque manner, were the limbs of a mannequin which had seen better days.

It reminded me that I had been looking for a tailor's dummy, now that I was getting more and more involved in the training of other handlers. I wanted the dummy so that I could re-construct search exercises.

We entered the shop which was still open despite the fact that there were workmen on the premises. I suppose it caused a stir to see a six foot copper with a big shaggy dog beside him in there. One of the builder's workmen looked a bit embarrassed when he recognised Ted from a previous experience but Ted did not let on that he knew him. Instead he asked for the manageress and asked if she had an old mannequin that he could buy. Of course, he had to explain what he wanted it for.

'You can have that one over there, but you'll have to take it now otherwise it will go in the skip. We are about to close the shop.'

Ted thanked her and without further ado went and picked up the naked lady who immediately broke into two, as they are supposed to. With the top half under one arm and the bottom part under the other arm, we made our way out of the shop and back into the High Street towards our van. I do not mind telling you, that van seemed a million miles away to me! You can imagine the looks and comments we got from the late afternoon shoppers. I do believe that Ted was enjoying it and having a good laugh. I must admit that I felt quite embarrassed when I saw how he was holding the two pieces.

Well you try it, and see just where your hands end up. One elderly chap made some comment which I did not quite catch but he was laughing. Ted stopped and said, 'I suppose you didn't witness this accident, did you, Sir?'

Please Believe Me

It was a bad time to try to track. There were many scents around and it was a very built up area although by this time it was beginning to get a little quieter.

Jubilee Clips Factory on the A2, Watling Street. Three men had broken in some hours earlier and had spent a long time in the hospitality area consuming alcohol meant for the entertaining of prospective customers. In their drunken haze they had left the building by smashing their way through a front window which led out onto Watling Street.

Ted put me into harness, as close as he dared to the broken glass which littered the area. The local police officers had not wandered about as they usually do so I was able to pick my way across the narrow strip of garden with its exhaust-burned shrubs and over the low wall onto the footpath off the main road. As I made my way slowly along the pavement, Ted kept me on a very short line. The scents were confusing on the narrow path. Cars went past quite quickly despite the presence of so many police in the area. The vacuum created at the rear of each vehicle drew the scent towards the road.

Very slowly, painstakingly to the watching police officers who did not understand the intricacies of the exercise, I picked out each footstep. Ted encouraged me, not put off by the lack of speed. He knew how difficult this was and that he was asking a lot of me.

The line went very taut as I turned towards the road, drawn there by a concentration of scent. On the road was an unopened packet of cigarettes, squashed flat by a passing car, but still bearing the odour of the last person to carry it.

Ted decided that the offenders had crossed the road near this point and he gathered up my line and waited for yet another car to pass. He cast me on the opposite side but still kept me on a very short line. At least now we were facing the on-coming traffic.

The men had crossed the main road at this point but they had not walked straight across as normal pedestrians do but had gone diagonally so it took me a few moments to find where they had mounted the opposite pavement. On I went, picking my way very slowly but definitely towards the next obstacle, a very large road junction. Something drew me to the wall. 'Good girl, Bess. What is it?'

You could not call them gardens really. The old terraced house had a low garden wall separating a concreted area from the public footpath. I tried the top of the wall with my nose. There was certainly something there. I put my front feet up onto the wall so that I could look over. Ted came forward.

'Oh, good girl. What a clever lady you are.' It was not the words that mattered, only the tone of voice.

Ted signalled to the other officers that I had found three bottles of whisky. They could collect them while he put me back to work. 'Another hundred yards and we'll be at that road junction. This track is difficult enough under these conditions but when we reach there my work will really be cut out.'

We got to the corner and Ted held tightly onto the line. I would really have to pull him to make sure that he knew that we were going the right way. No point going on a wild goose chase. Funny term, that. 'Come on now, concentrate. Yes, there it is.' They had not turned right but had gone across the side street. I pulled and Ted was just starting to follow me when a car screamed to a halt beside him. The policeman shouted through the open window.

'Three men have just been seen in Luton rec. We'll give you a lift.'

Ted bundled me, still in harness, into the rear seat of the car. We were thrown back as the car accelerated rapidly before we were settled in. Into the side road and off towards the rec. How I wished I could speak. I knew that the offenders had crossed the road.

We got to the rec to find that another police car was already there. The two drivers spoke to each other through the open windows. I heard one say, 'Yes. There were three men but they were O.K. They had just finished the late shift at the factory up the road.'

I cannot repeat what Ted said as he asked the driver to get us back to the junction. When we arrived back to where I had been so rudely interrupted, there was a uniformed officer standing on the pavement. At his feet was the crumpled form of a drunken man.

'Oh. I thought you'd all finished up here so I thought I'd have a look round. Chummy here was sound asleep behind that car over there. He has got five bottles of scotch and a load of fags.'

Was the constable gloating, I unkindly thought.

I was furious. Oh, not with Bess but with myself. I knew that she had worked extremely hard for me but I had allowed myself to get caught up in the excitement of the frivolous sighting of the three innocent men. I knew that if I had allowed her to continue tracking, she would have taken me to where the man was hiding with his loot.

We completed a search of the car park but there was no trace of the other men or any more property. Ted immediately took me to the industrial park along the road and laid me a short training track. I fairly rushed round this one as it was so easy and I enjoyed the praise and encouragement from him. As I flopped down beside the kiddies shoe which was the last article, placed conspicuously for me to find, he exploded into a game with me. It was in reparation for what had happened earlier and I really made the most of the fuss. I knew that inwardly he was still cursing himself. I had worked hard but he had let me down and experience should have taught him better.

Fort-titude

Fort Horsted at Chatham was used by Rochester Motor Company for storing and preparing new cars for sale.

We arrived to be met by the local constable, a detective from the C.I.D., and the managing director from the car firm. We stood there, me beside Ted, tracking harness over his shoulder.

'There are at least two of them. They have been driving new cars around like stock-cars. There's no end of damage.' There was a tone of despair as the detective related the tale.

'We'll do what we can for you. Take me to where they were last seen.' I was pleased that Ted included me in the conversation.

We all walked across the bridge into the fort. I could not resist putting my nose to the ground, such is the effect that the sight of the tracking harness has on me. 'Not yet Bess,' Ted whispered.

The C.I.D. officer stayed on the bridge because it was the only lawful way for anyone to get in or out of the fort.

The damage inside was awful. Cars were smashed into each other, into walls and one was even precariously on its side near the drop into the moat. Somebody had been very lucky to get out of that one.

'This is where we think they were last but we're not sure,' said one of the officers.

Whilst he was talking I was surveying the wanton destruction of these brand new vehicles and perhaps thinking of my ancient estate car.

'Come on, Bess.' My foreleg lifted automatically as Tea bent over to put the harness on me. 'About time too, it's been in sight for ages now.'

I kept Bess on a very short line. There was a tremendous amount of broken glass around but more worrying was the proximity of the dried up moat. The walls were of sheer concrete and the drop must have been about fifty feet.

'No, nothing there. Let's try over here.' I pulled on the abnormally short line. Ted turned on the spot and held the line at arms length to allow me to work as freely as he dared whilst keeping me out of danger.

I pulled as I picked up the scent. Ted held back slightly as he called over his shoulder. 'Any of you been over here?' I fairly dragged Ted away from the others as someone replied, 'No, that's not us.' The pressure on the line relaxed a little as Ted increased his pace to stay with me.

I still kept her on a very short line. That dried up moat was getting too close for comfort yet I was sure she was right.

'Good girl, Bess,' he cooed. The scent drew me away from the edge of that drop after a short while. The terrain was very overgrown. 'Ted to Les,' Ted breathed into his radio. 'We are coming towards you. They must be heading towards the bridge where you are.'

Suddenly, they were in front of us. They must have been sitting up hiding from us. We had rounded a clump of brambles and there they were right on the edge of the moat.

'Hey. Stand still,' shouted Ted, knowing that the two youths had seen us. They stopped momentarily. I was on my hind legs screaming to be released. Come on Ted. Let me go and I'll stop them for you. Hurry.

The youths ran right round the edge of the moat, demonstrating that they knew the area very well. Bess would have stopped their flight quite easily but it was just too dangerous both for her and for them.

Ted wound up the line so that it was being used as a lead and we ran after them. Sure enough, they ran right onto the bridge with Ted and I just behind them.

They looked and saw the C.I.D. officer in front of them and realised that it was all over. Their half hour of fun was to cost them dearly.

It was rare to arrest offenders in front of the owner of the damaged property. He was overjoyed.

He was even more pleased when we were able to find out how the youths had gained entry into this place. After all this is a fort! They had lowered themselves on a hosepipe down the outer moat wall, walked across the dried up bottom and squeezed through a service hatch in the inner wall. They even left one of their jackets there as a marker.

Bess's Notoriety

Duty at Gillingham football ground was a pastime that Ted enjoyed. He liked the chance to carry out a lot of public relations as well as me being a good deterrent to would-be trouble makers.

Before the match started and again at half-time, we would walk around the edge of the pitch. He encouraged me to put my front feet up onto the low retaining wall so that the children could reach me. Oh. Do not get me wrong. There are many hooligans who know the other side of my nature.

One Saturday afternoon, Ted was doing his PR bit and I was enjoying the attention of the children while he spoke to their parents. We moved along and I put my feet up, just as a little boy looked over the wall. We met face to face and I could not resist giving him a wet lick. He turned to his father, who was laughing, and said, 'Dad, I've just been tasted by a bear.' I have heard Ted say, in the past, that it is nice to have a dog that he can trust. One that he can switch on and off, just like a car's ignition. I think that there is a compliment in there somewhere.

On another occasion, at the same venue, we were doing our friendly bit when the radio crackled into life. 'Take a look ahead of you, Ted.' We looked towards the vaguely notorious Rainham End, and there, hanging over the retaining wall, was a homemade banner which read, 'Bess bites yer legs.'

Ted turned and walked the other way. I could feel the laughter in his body. My fame was spreading!

Murder on the Great Lines

Sunday morning and I was dozing in the back of the van. The early morning sun-light reached me through the glass. We were on day shift but had left home early. Ted was now in Chatham police station. I could see some activity across the other side of the car park, where a small ornamental wall separates it from the gardens which border the police station.

A police officer was crouching down beside another person who was lying on the grass by the wall. Then I saw Ted come out of the back door with two other officers and they ran to where the person was lying. I livened up then, as Ted was in sight, but still I could do nothing but watch.

Yet another officer came out with a blanket. Ted ran across towards the van and I knew that work was inevitable.

I was in the chain as quick as lightening and I looked up at my tracking harness as it bounced on Ted's shoulder, when we ran across the yard.

We passed the person on the ground and I could see that it was a young girl. There was blood seeping from the many stab wounds on the upper part of her body. We stopped momentarily and I was mesmerised by the ever-increasing blood patches as they soaked into the blanket.

The officers were working frantically as they waited for the ambulance. We ran across the ornamental gardens to a small gateway which led out onto the Great Lines, which was basically a large tract of common land. There was a small pool of blood on the step in the gateway. Ted took a piece of wax crayon, normally used to mark the road at the scene of road traffic accidents, and made a ring round the glistening spots.

Now it was up to me. I was in harness and tracking but this time it was different. It was easy for me to tell which way a track should go, and I told Ted by my actions that we should be heading back towards the girl. No. He encouraged me, on this occasion, to go the other way. This was a back-track. He wanted to find the point where the young lady was attacked.

I picked my way along the chalk and grass path which led in the general direction of the war memorial towering in the distance in the middle of the common land.

Every so often Ted would tell me to lie down as he marked further puddles of blood on the path. It was difficult enough tracking like this. It was a back-track, which in itself is not easy as it is against all training, but to be stopping all the time was not helpful to my concentration.

The path became tarmac and blood spots shone more frequently. Ted had to mark each one he saw in order to preserve the area before they dried up and were lost forever.

Tumbling along the path, lifted by the breeze, was a bundle of white tissues. Ted weighted them down with a stone, as they too were blood stained.

The tentative track turned off the path and into a small copse. It was no longer a question of tracking now because there were so many tissues lying about. Ted unclipped my line and together we searched the copse. He weighted down several more blood-soaked tissues.

Back to the path and with tracking line back on, we made our way slowly along. More blood spots confirmed that we were right. 'Wait! What's that?' Just off the path, a concentration of scent. I laid down, my tail moving from side to side very slowly. 'Good girl. Stay.'

Ted approached, along the line. It was a lady's shoe. He marked an arrow on the tarmac indicating where the object was. 'Track on Bess. You're doing fine,' Ted cajoled.

A few yards on, another shoe, in plain view this time, in the middle of the path. A larger pool of blood. More tissues.

Then things started to go my way a little. There was another scent leading off the path and up the grassy bank. This time we were travelling in the same direction as the person making it.

Our speed increased as I pulled up the bank towards the monument. Come on Ted, we can get this person.

A hundred yards or so from the path, I lay down. Ted came up and found the reason I had done so. A pair of sunglasses, in a case. They had not been there long because they were bone dry and the grass was quite wet from the overnight rain.

'Oh, good girl. Track on.' I charged to the full extent of my tracking line, eager to get on. Ted did not come with me and my forward motion came to an abrupt halt. He groaned, and I then saw the problem.

Everything was against us that day. Coming towards us was a very large group of people. They had with them dogs of all different shapes and colours. It was a sponsored walk and little did they know that they were obliterating the scent of a killer!

Ted praised me as he took me out of harness very quickly. The sunglasses were safely in his pocket in a plastic bag. A stick marked where they had been found.

We went back to the path, to where Ted had marked the blood and the second shoe. He put me on the lead and very carefully we had a look round. There was an area of flattened grass on the opposite side of the path. There was also something white. Ted put me down on the path and walked across to it. It was the collar of a blouse. That had not been there long either, and was also blood-stained. We had found the scene of the attack.

Some people, stragglers from the sponsored walk who had taken a wrong path, came towards us. Ted sent them back the way they had come. No one, as far as he was concerned, was coming through that area before the scenes of crime officers had done their job.

I lay there while he made notes and plans in his pocket book, knowing that they would be needed later.

We waited, turning the odd person away from the scene, until Ted was relieved by the other officers who had come to find him.

He talked to me as we walked back towards the police station. We had done all we could but he wished we could have done more.

I lay in the corner of the C.I.D. office while Ted made a proper list of our finds up there on the common. He completed his statement. The sunglasses were handed over to the scenes of crime officer who thanked him for preserving them for him.

I know that if you were to search Ted at any time of the day or night when he is on duty, you will find that he always carries two pieces of equipment. A piece of wax crayon wrapped up, and some polythene exhibit bags.

The young lady died in hospital. She was eighteen, married, and was on her way to Rochester Cathedral where she was a bell-ringer and chorister.

A man was later arrested for her murder and is now serving a life sentence.

This incident is recounted in 'Clues to Murder' by Tom Tullett, published by the Bodley Head Ltd, 1986.

One Makes Three

Night Duty Headquarters security patrol was never a duty that Ted and I liked. It was just a question of checking people who were seen moving about the complex, who would invariably turn out to be police officers either coming to work or going home. We also had to check buildings to make sure that police-men had done their jobs properly before going home. I did, however, get a chance to see the girls in operations room for a lot of fuss while Ted had a cup of tea.

The van was parked on the square and of course we had to be at the far end of the complex when the personal radio crackled into life.

'Could you attend Berwyn Grove? It's only down the road from you and the local dog's engaged.' We ran to the van, both relieved for something con-structive to do. Three men had been seen tampering with vehicles. We were obviously going to be the first car on the scene so as Ted drove into the Grove he switched off all the lights and just coasted down the slope, with the engine just ticking over.

The adrenalin was flowing and I looked over Ted's shoulder. Even I saw the dark figure run across the road under a streetlamp in the distance. I was thrown against the rear of the van as Ted accelerated hard and switched on all the lights.

Hand brake on and he was out of the van before it had stopped moving. The back doors opened as he shouted the usual challenge after the fleeing man, who was now running up the road we had driven down.

'Stand still or I'll send the police dog.' I fairly screamed as my feet would not gain purchase straight away. There he was, going across the gardens. Round the corner. I caught up with him easily. He was worried and looking over his shoulder for me. I took him on the elbow, my teeth grazing the skin as I took hold of his jacket. It tore, but it held. 'Don't struggle, you fool. You can't win.'

The man gave up his struggling so I let go but kept a wary eye on him. I did not like the smell of him. Ted came round the corner. The torch shone on the man and I could see the dark patch, spreading on the front of his trousers. He had wet himself. 'I'll make a bet that this one gets taken away in another police vehicle, if I know Ted.'

The Maidstone car arrived as we reached the van. 'There are two more somewhere. I'll do a search, if you'll take care of this one.' I would have won my bet. The prisoner was safely ensconced in the car. 'Seek on, Bess.'

I raced off into the gardens where he had first seen the man. I almost skidded to a halt as I raced through the scent picture of a screwdriver lying in the grass. 'I know he's given me the word to search for a person but I expect he'll want the screwdriver too.' I picked up the tool and took it to where Ted was waiting with another officer. 'Oh, good girl! We'll save that one for the scenes of crime.'

I finished searching that garden. Nothing more in this one but there was something that was drawing me into the next one. It was only something on the breeze. 'Go on then, seek on.' Ted had seen my reaction. 'There you are.' The youth had squeezed himself into a very narrow space between a shed and a wall. I was not going in there. I barked like mad. It brought Ted running and caused a few more lights to go on.

'Come on out mate. You haven't a chance.' Ted put his light on the face of the person and I could see that he was only about sixteen.

The youth struggled out and was taken away by the Maidstone police officers. I was put in to search for the third person but I could not find anyone else.

There were several officers there by now, and Ted gathered them all together in the front garden of one of the houses.

'Look, take my keys. One of you drive my van and all make a show of driving away. I'll give it another twenty minutes or so.'

We sat quietly in the darkened open porch and listened to the sound of the car engines as they became quieter. I relished the feel of his arm across my back as he stroked my chest.

It is very strange how things soon get back to normal after such a disturbance. One by one the lights of the disturbed households went off. A cat padded past, unaware of our presence. A fox too, but he winded us and stopped dead before gliding away to call back from a distance. Suddenly, a fence rattled from way up the road. 'Quiet girl,' Ted whispered, his hand unnecessarily holding my muzzle.

Down the road came a man. He had the shock of his life when we stepped out of the shadows close to him. I growled instinctively knowing that he was up to no good. Ted switched on his radio and within a minute there were the Maidstone car and my van.

The three men had broken into four cars in the area and had also committed a burglary at Loose school. The proceeds from that break had been hidden in a hedgerow for later collection but the youth showed us where it all was.

A nice clear-up and very much better than plodding around Headquarters.

One old fashioned look ('Chatham, Rochester & Gillingham News')

You Can Take a Dog to Water

Dogs of all shapes and sizes. Dogs of all breeds and colours. Owners as varied as their dogs. Some men. Some women. A dog show at Gillingham Park in aid of the RSPCA. All aspects of working dogs were there. Ted and I were there representing the police and to talk to members of the public and to answer their questions, 'What breed is it?' being the favourite.

The fête was opened by the celebrity, Mr David Jacobs, and after the opening ceremony he walked around to see the various stalls and exhibits. A young lady newspaper reporter asked him if he would mind posing with the police dog — Me!

I did not mind sitting there beside him as he crouched down at a kiddies' paddling pool but I did mind when he tried to push my head down to make me drink. Still, one old-fashioned look and he stopped and made do with lifting water up to me on the palm of his hand as though giving me a drink.

After that, the young lady reporter asked Ted for some detail for her article. He duly obliged! Then the inevitable question.

'And what breed is she?' She obviously did not see the tweaking at the corners of his mouth and the twinkle in his eye as he launched into his reply.

'She's an Afghan Needle Hound, especially imported because there was once an illegal abortion carried out in Kent and a size ten knitting needle was used. She can only find size tens so we are going to import some more hounds to find other sizes, just in case it happens again.'

The young lady was writing furiously in shorthand trying to keep up with him until someone, who was listening nearby, sniggered. The pause was measurable and then the pages were ripped off her pad, screwed up and she tried to stuff them down Ted's neck. I fleetingly thought about protecting him, but what the heck, he deserved all he got. That sense of humour of his.

The Strood Prowler

The Medway Towns had been plagued by a man for more than two years. He was a burglar who, if he found a woman alone in the house, would indecently assault her as well as ransack the home. So notorious was he that the police formed special units to try to catch him, but to no avail. The local press dubbed him 'The Notorious Strood Prowler'.

I am sure that we had been tracking the same man many times at the scenes of different crimes. Each time he had given us the slip, either by his cunning, or just good fortune on his part, bad on ours.

I was dozing in the van whilst Ted was in Chatham police station. The door opened and he got in.

Another policeman got into the passenger seat. 'I think I know the address, it's up Lordswood area.' Out of the yard and into the Brook. I felt that tingle of anticipation of work and I looked over Ted's shoulder as we drove quite rapidly to that area.

'Good girl, Bess,' he said, as our eyes met in the interior mirror. He stopped the van outside the address. They both left the vehicle and it became quiet, with only the pip...pip of the force radio, as I turned first to look out of the back window and then out of the front. Nothing.

Within minutes, the back door of the van opened and I jumped down as Ted reached inside for the tracking gear. We walked swiftly to an alleyway about three doors down from the attacked house.

Into the harness and off we went. This was all hard surface and I had to be careful and pick my way along the rapidly diminishing scent trail.

Out of the alley, diagonally across the road. Into another alley. Although this is a fairly modern estate, it is riddled with back alleys and short cuts, and the person I was following seemed to know the area quite well. Out of the alley, I turned left along the footpath. Good job it was early hours of the morning otherwise this area would have been alive with people.

'Wait a minute. An open garden gate. Just check that again. Yes, there it is.' I pulled in to the garden path, the tracking line rasping against the gate post. 'Is she right?' whispered the other officer. 'We're O.K.' Ted replied.

Down the garden path. The front door was wide open, the door mat was propping it back. Ted leaned back on the line, stopping my forward motion. The pressure eased and on I went. Through the open door and along the darkened passage. Through the back door which had been kept open by the same method.

'Make a note of this address. We'll have to come back,' hissed Ted. I nearly pulled his arm from its socket, as the scent dragged me down the garden and out of the open rear gate.

On we went, across roads and down alleys, which were proving difficult because of where numerous people had walked their dogs.

We then entered a small wood. The track became easier but I could see the lights of the shopping centre ahead. Ted trotted to catch up with me a little, so that he could gather in some of the thirty foot line to prevent it tangling around trees or bushes.

The track led straight through the wood and out onto the edge of the car park. More effort needed now. No rushing from Ted, although the other officer was impatient and wanted to run on.

'Track on Bessie. Good girl.' I had just picked up the scent again when Ted said to the other man, 'Look over there.'

A car was being pushed across the car park. One man was at the driver's door, steering, and another was pushing at the rear. 'I'll get the one at the back. You grab the driver.'

We, all three, pounced at the right moment and I indicated my presence by barking. The two men gave up quite easily.

The other officer searched their vehicle and came out with a plastic bag full of purses and wallets. One of the purses was from the house that I had tracked through. The owners did not even know yet that they had been burgled.

'There's no end of stuff in here, Ted,' said the other officer as he emerged from the car. Neither Ted nor the other officer realised at this stage that they had at last caught 'The Notorious Strood Prowler'.

The man and his accomplice were sentenced to four and a half years imprisonment having admitted to twenty-five burglaries and many nasty assaults on women.

It's That Car Again

The car used by the Strood prowler was an ancient Morris Oxford, and about two weeks after we had arrested him and his cohort, our attention was, once again, drawn to that same vehicle.

I was off duty and out for our last walk of the day. We were making our way through the car park by Rainham railway station. It was almost ten o'clock and there were just a few vehicles left in the large car park.

We were making for my favourite recreation ground and the rough ground alongside the railway track, when Ted stopped.

My attention was drawn to a car which I recognised straight away as belonging to the Strood Prowler. It could not have been him in it as he was still in custody. The Morris Oxford was being driven slowly around the car park. Every so often it stopped with its headlights on full beam. I had not realised it at first, but each time it stopped the headlights were shining onto a model of Ford car.

We moved into the shadows of the pavilion on the edge of the recreation ground. I sat quietly beside Ted, sensing the adrenalin in his body. Work was imminent.

The Morris slid into a space beside a Ford Capri. From where I was, I could not see anything so we stayed put. The Morris moved out within a minute or two and recommenced circling the car park, a little like a shark looking for prey. Again it slipped neatly into the space between two vehicles, one of which was a Ford Escort.

This time I was in a good position to see exactly what was going on. The driver of the Morris slid over onto his front passenger seat and reached through the open window. He unlocked the driver's door of the Ford and clambered across into the driver's seat. His feet did not even touch the ground.

The man was very engrossed when Ted reached into the Ford and took hold of his collar. The radio, recently removed from its bracket, fell to the floor.

'Hello, my friend. This is just not your day is it?' Ted said. I growled and pulled towards the man but Ted restrained me. The man had nowhere to go anyway.

We escorted him over to the fish and chip shop on the corner and the proprietor rang the local police station for Ted. Once again we found ourselves at the police station doing paperwork off duty.

What the Dickens?

The building was derelict. Lath and plaster walls that had seen better days. Bare wooden floors stained by water allowed in by previous raids on the lead on the roof.

'Come on out. The place is surrounded. You might as well give up. We know you're in there.' Ted did not need to tell them that he had a dog with him. I made sure that they knew as I was wound up by the tone of his challenge. 'Go seek, Bess.'

The chain slipped as I was first directed down into the rain-soaked basement. It took only seconds to make sure that there was no one down there. Ted's arm extended as he directed me onto the ground floor. Rubbish left by people sleeping rough moved and rustled as I rushed from room to room looking for the men suspected of stripping lead from the roof.

Ted followed me in. He was satisfied that there was nobody on this level. Again, I followed the way his arm was pointing as he re-directed me up the steep, dirty stairs.

This house had seen better days. It was only a few doors along from Charles Dickens' early home in Ordnance Terrace.

Someone had been on this floor; their scent was strong. A small pile of lead placed in the corner of one room for later collection. From room to room I rushed. Nothing. I came to the bathroom door which was tightly shut. I stopped. If I put my head onto one side a little I could hear the sound of some-one breathing. There was a crackle of flaked plaster on the floor as a nervously moved foot crushed it. I put my nose to the crack at the bottom of the door and a deep intake of breath confirmed what I already knew. There was someone in there.

A quick scratch at the door and then I let Ted know that I had found someone. A loud bark. He came up the stairs. 'Where is he then? Good girl. O.K. Mate. The dog is secure. Now come out.'

The door opened a few inches and a man peered out. This made me bark even more and I strained against the lead. 'Go on Ted, let me have another go at that door.'

'Hello, Mr Wright. Have you got him on a lead?' Why do they always assume that police dogs are 'he's'?

'Oh. It's you, Billy. Come on out.' It was like a reunion. Ted had arrested this petty thief on three previous occasions.

He sent the man down the stairs to the waiting police officers. 'Right,' he shouted. 'We've got Billy. You might as well come down now.'

There was a slight pause and then there was a noise from up in the attic. The hatch moved and another man appeared. He was filthy and looked petrified when he saw me. 'Keep that dog on a lead. I'm coming down.' We had heard that voice before, and almost the very same words, except that his language had improved. He was one of the two who had been stealing diesel fuel from the building site so many years earlier.

The two were made to carry their lean pickings of lead out to the waiting police cars which were to take them off to yet another court appearance.

Bluebell Hill Yet Again

Ted was assisting with an incident at the Medway Accident Centre when the call came in.

At top speed we made our way to the Maidstone end of Bluebell Hill. Ted stopped and got out. Through the front grille I could see several police cars. A car with a roof rack was almost off the road into a field.

'I'm afraid we have thrashed about a bit Ted, because we were close enough to chase them. We caught one but there are two more out there somewhere.'

Ted was buckling up my harness almost before I had put my foreleg through it. It had become second nature by now.

Again the familiar feel of the line being paid out and touching my back momentarily before Ted lifted it clear.

The scents were confusing around the car so Ted moved further away. He cast me in a large circle. There was a lot of sorting out to be done if we were to help the Maidstone officers find the outstanding offenders.

'Nothing, Nothing. Fox. No nothing. Ah Mr Rabbit was here a short time ago. Leave it. Nothing. What's that?'

The line almost burned Ted's fingers as he gently checked me. I lunged forward. At last the human scent I had been looking for. I wished I could speak. I would have told him that gypsies were involved.

'We're away, Skipper.' Ted called over his shoulder to officers who were obviously doubting our ability. Across the ploughed field I picked my way, and through the hedge on the far side. Into the orchard where the track became easier to follow.

Ted would know from experience and my actions that I was tracking two men. Body language means a lot between dog and man and man and dog. We read each other like a book.

'Ah. Turning right, are we? To the barbed wire fence.'

I squeezed under the lower strand, leaving black fur on the barbs. I hate the stuff.

'Down Bessie.' I lay down with my nose working frantically at the odour on the ground in front of me. 'Come on Ted.' He clambered over the fence. 'Track on. Good girl.'

He did not really have to say that, but it becomes a habit. I was away, meandering slightly as I checked the parallel trails of the two men. These are devious people and I have learned that they do not like police dogs. They get up to all sorts of things to get us off the scent. Crossing rivers, climbing trees, back tracking on themselves. All sorts of antics which, by experience, can be sorted out.

Across the field to yet another barbed wire fence. Yet more fur left behind. The corn stubble stabbed at my nose causing small bubbles of blood to form. One quick lick and they were gone. Turning now.

These people were unfamiliar with this area and they were making their way guided by the lights of Aylesford in the distance. Another barbed wire fence, more fur. 'Down Bess.' I waited for the command to track on. Instead, I heard what seemed to be a tremendous crash and a grunt from Ted as he hit the ground. The top strand of barbed wire had snapped as he tested his weight on it. I went back to him. His left leg was doubled up beneath him. I could smell the blood where the barbed wire had ripped across his back and arms. His shirt was torn to shreds and was covered with blood.

I stayed there for what seemed ages. It was very rare for police officers to follow a dog handler on a track of this nature. One — dog handlers do not very often encourage them to do so. Two — they can rarely keep us with us.

On this occasion it was fortunate that the sergeant and one of the constables from the scene had followed and had managed to keep pace too.

They gingerly pulled the wire away from Ted and he sat there, not daring to move the left leg from under him. It was really at a strange angle. By their torchlight, I could see that he was ashen and blood was still seeping from the scores on his back and arms.

He managed a weak grin, as he said, 'Now I know how Steve McQueen must have felt, in the Great Escape.' That meant nothing to me.

'Give us a hand, fellers.' The two officers lifted Ted to his feet. He stood there for a moment not daring to move, then bent his leg a few times. Stamping his feet as though trying to shake the pain away, he picked up the line. 'Come on, Bess. Let's have another go.' Away I tracked, conscious that I was pulling quite a weight as Ted tried to keep up with me. 'Come on Ted. I know they're near.'

Into another orchard. With head up, I fairly charged forward. The musty stench of unwashed bodies and clothing was strong.

The two gypsies had no fight in them. They had run nearly two miles over rough ground and, because of the delay when I fell, they had presumed that pursuit had given up. As the handcuffs went on, I think that they were relieved. The sergeant and the constable led the two men towards the nearest road, and by radio, arranged for a car to meet them.

Ted sat on the ground and made a terrific fuss of me as he took me out of harness and rolled up the line. He was obviously hurt and I was careful, but I so wanted to respond to his praise and to be close to him.

Another car picked up Ted and me and took us back to the van, way in the distance. His knee by this time was swollen like a balloon and he could not drive. Someone obliged by driving us home.

I did not know it at that stage but that fall was to alter my whole life.

CHAPTER FOUR

Frustrations

I was off sick for more than nine months. I had damaged the ligaments of my left knee. I spent several periods in hospital and was in plaster for a long time after being allowed home.

I had to go to Stockbury kennels each time he went away for weeks at a time. Whenever he did come home, one of his colleagues, knowing how much he missed me, collected me from the kennels and took me home. He would also call each day to take me out for a run. It was very nice of him and I enjoyed it a lot but it was not the same as the long walks with Ted, who sat with his plastered leg up for weeks on end. I did get to spend a lot more time indoors with him and Jan, though.

Towards the end of his period of injury, it was decided, by whoever makes these decisions, that I would be retired because of my age and the fact that I had not had any continuation training for so long. I knew that I could still work but they thought they knew best.

Ted was out of plaster and was able to walk me gently. Instead of walking long distances, we would drive out into the country and then walk. Smashing.

One day a van arrived and a seven month old pup was delivered. Ted wanted another bitch and I greeted her and welcomed her to the household. 'Let us just get one thing clear. The proper bed is mine. You have the one in the box. O.K.!'

She was Kenpol Duchess, immediately to become 'Jo'. She had been bred at Stockbury kennels and I was quite surprised that I had not met her when I was there for all those weeks.

Jo was black and tan in colour, smooth-coated and she already shone quite nicely. The thing I really noticed was the size of her ears. Well I would, wouldn't I?

They stood up straight and were even larger than usual, just to rub it in.

I now knew how Rajah felt when I had arrived on the scene so many years ago. Pleased to see her and have company but also realising that she was here to take over from me eventually. I now knew how Rajah felt when I was taken out on environmental training and he was left behind. It was all happening to me now.

Because I was retired, I now belonged to Jan and Ted and I became their pet. Whilst Ted was out getting Jo used to things, Jan took me out for walks. It was not the same and I had to adjust my pace to hers. Jan has rheumatoid arthritis and has had many operations on her legs. I know how she feels, too.

It was agreed that I could go back to work on light duties. My leg had not healed as yet, and there was some doubt that it ever would. I was very fed up and wanted to get back into the swing of things. I had completed Jo's environmental

Jo when eight months old

Raggin' tuition for Jo.

training in my own time anyway. A basic course was already running and it was decided that I could join that.

I was very pleased to learn that the course was being carried out locally so it meant that Ted would not be away for weeks at a time as he was with me.

Ted passed out as operational with Jo and occasionally he took me out to work with him for a ride round. It was a bit like when I was a pup and I had to stay in the van while Ted worked Rajah, only now he was working Jo. I felt a bit left out of it. I could still do the job, although, if I was honest, getting over some of the fences would be a bit difficult nowadays. My colitis was playing up a bit, too.

Jo, again, was an excellent tracking dog. It must be something that Ted does right in his training. However, her manwork was suspect! She tried hard but was not powerful enough and it was a little bit beyond her. Ted had to be careful how he dealt with incidents now because he would not get the backing from her. I hoped he realised.

A Million For Your Job?

It all came to a head one night when I was in the spare cage of the van.

An alarm sounded at the girls' school at the top of Chatham Hill. When we got there, Jo and I could not gain entry because of the high spiked railings surrounding the place. The keyholder had to come from a long way off and would be a long time.

111

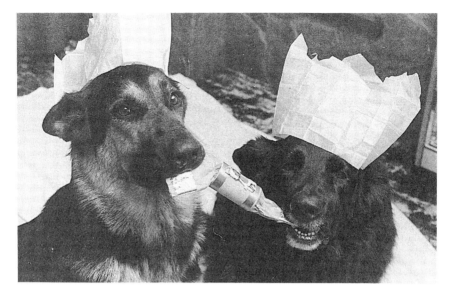

Jo and I celebrate Christmas

Jo overdoes it!

I had been to a burglary at the same school with Bess some years ago. That time we had tracked along an alleyway which led down to Beacon Road, before the scent had been fouled by people walking towards us. I told the local officers that while they waited for the keyholder, I would go and sit up at the end of the alley just in case the same route of escape was used this time.

Opposite the alley in Beacon Road is a private coach depot. On the main building are arc lights which illuminate the coach park but leave an inky darkness right up against the building itself. I parked in this shadow and there we remained, unseen to passers by.

We had only been there for a few minutes when we heard voices. Ted sat still. Jo's ears became even larger. I lifted my head.

The voices were coming from Church Hill which is in the opposite direction to the alley where I was half expecting people to appear from.

I watched the two men walk up Church Hill and into Beacon Road. They were obviously up to no good from their actions, but were completely divorced from the alarm at the school. I could see them clearly when they looked in our direction, but the arc lights dazzled them and they had no idea that we were there. They ran quietly across the road and into the building site opposite.

Ted sat still but fingered the lead which lay on the front passenger seat within easy reach for when he had to get out fast.

One man re-appeared with an armful of house bricks. He stood, waiting for his colleague.

Suddenly, he was illuminated by the headlights of a coach returning late to its depot. The man darted back behind the stack of bricks.

I was now in a quandary. The coach would turn into the yard with its headlights on and it would show up our van with all its markings.

He slid out of the van and round to the back. Jo's head went into the chain. They were then lost to view and I spun to look out of the front window again.

The coach started making its turn, headlights full on. Ted stepped out and gestured to the driver who seemed to understand right away and turned all his lights off. Ted and Jo ran along the side of the coach using it as cover as they advanced onto the building site and they disappeared from my view.

I was frustrated. What was going on? There was a lot of shouting.

It seemed an age before the driver's door of the van opened and the interior light came on. Hang on. That's not Ted. It was the coach driver. I suppose that I should have barked at the stranger in my van but for some unknown reason, I did not. The driver looked around in wonderment for a few seconds and then picked up the radio handset.

'Hello...hello. Is there anybody up there?' he said, nervously, and obviously not knowing anything about radio procedure.

The radio operator in the police operations centre was excellent. She made all authorised callers stand by and told the coach driver to go ahead.

'You'd better get someone up here quick. Your mate doesn't half need help,' he told her.

Jo and me . . . I still think that her ears are too big!

Within minutes there were blue lights flashing in the area, but it seemed an age before I saw Ted and Jo again. Ted was helped back towards the van by two police officers. Blood was streaming from the cuts above his eyes which were already beginning to close. His nose was bleeding and his chin was cut.

One of the men stealing building materials had seen me coming. As I rounded the stack of building blocks I was met by a house brick in the face. Quite a fight took place but the only thing I could think of was that I must not be knocked to the ground. I had seen the boots they were wearing. Seems silly now!

I shouted at the top of my voice to the coach driver to use the radio in the van. Jo in the meantime was beside me barking and making all the right noises but doing very little else. This was all beyond her capabilities.

The two men ran off down Church Hill and I sent Jo to chase them. This time she did as she should and went after them. Church Hill, although not very long is very steep. Jo caught up with one of the men and in the bad light, tripped him up. I then fell over him.

I had taken quite a beating and that fall just about finished me. I looked up just in time to see the two men run into a small block of maisonettes. The next thing I remembered was leaning over the bonnet of a police Range-Rover.

All the residents of the flats were roused until the two men were traced. I was quite pleased to see that one of them was holding his head where my torch had connected during the fight.

I was about to get into the ambulance when I saw the coachdriver standing by the roadside.

114

'Thanks Mate,' I said, as normally as I could through thickening lips.
The driver replied, 'I wouldn't have your bloody job for a million pounds. No.
Make that a million and one pounds.'
I tried to smile but I doubt if it looked very much like a smile from where he
was.

The following day Ted was at home, nursing his injuries, when a sergeant called to see how he was. I was curled up beside his chair when I heard Ted say, 'Jo was absolutely useless. She let me down terribly. She just does not have it in her.'

Take My Lead, Jo

Jan had not been home for several days and Ted took me out in the van with him when he was working with Jo. I did not enjoy it quite as much nowadays. Oh, I liked being with them and feeling the presence of Jo as we lay side by side with only the wire mesh between us, but I found it difficult to get into the van. Even though I took one almighty leap, Ted still had to give me a welcome boost until I was right in.

One day, before he put his uniform jacket on, he walked me on the lead along to the old lady who lives nearby. I was glad it was not far and that he was not in a hurry. She has Stefan, an Alsatian, with whom I have been friendly for years. He is not as old as I am but is very staid in his ways, and did not expect me to chase around with him. In his own way he welcomed us.

Ted made sure that I was happy before leaving me to go off to work with Jo.

I had not been there very long when I started to feel strange and unwell. I was in front of the fire but felt cold. I was lying flat on my side yet I felt that I was up in the air looking down on myself.

Everything seemed muddled. I remember being carried out of the van and into the vet's. I had a needle in my leg. I felt hands on my chest and stomach. I began to feel a little warmer and became aware of the tube and the fluid passing through it into my leg. I had another needle in my side...

I woke up at home with Ted and Jo. I knew that I had been to the vet's because of the taste in my mouth and the smell on my coat. I tried to lick most of that off. Jo came and sniffed me and went to lie down on the far side of the room.

That night I was restless. Ted spent most of the long hours sitting up with me. I had long since finished sleeping outside in the kennel. That was for younger and fitter dogs like Jo. I now had my own blanket beside Ted's chair where I was quite content.

The following day I felt much better and was able to go out in the van with Ted and Jo when they went to work.

During a spare moment we drove into Rochester Airport and I walked in the sunshine while Jo ran and exercised. I lay down and watched her chase her stick. It was nice to see her run where I used to run.

Friday and Ted was on rest day. Jo and I were left indoors when he went out. He had not been gone too long before we heard voices. He was back and had Jan with him. I had not seen her for so long.

The back door opened and there they both were. Ted was helping Jan up the steps on her crutches. Both Jo and I welcomed her, Jo perhaps more exuberantly than I, until Ted made us both go in. When Jan was comfortable on the settee we were both encouraged to go and see her. I was so pleased that we were a family again.

It is night time and I feel tired out. I am indoors beside Ted's chair. I need to go out in the garden. Ted takes me but I stagger and almost fall. It is all such an effort. Please help me back to the house.

It is late and I only want to sleep. Jo is in her kennel settled for the night. Ted is speaking on the telephone. 'Not another call out?' I stupidly think. I feel light-headed.

He is on his knees gathering me to him. I am embarrassed by being picked up like this but I have always liked the warmth and feel of his body.

Ted carries me through the house and I am placed gently on my rug which is now just inside the bedroom door. Was that a tear? He stays until I settle. Jan is already in bed but not asleep. I'm glad she's home at last.

I am on my side. It is the most comfortable position. It is dark though I see things most clearly. Jo is swimming with my brothers and sisters. Rajah comes running but I cannot quite remember what he looks like. I look down and I see myself. Why am I so cold in this warm, warm place? My mind is a turmoil. My tracking harness bites into my shoulders as I pull hard to tell Ted which way the man went. Who went? Where am I going? Thick cloud approaches. The smell of the clover is thick and heavy on the air. Jo's beautiful ears. Watch out for that rake, Ted. Tomorrow we'll walk for miles. I just have to rest tonight and I'll be fine...

I Could Not Have Asked For More

When going to work with Jo it was not always possible to take Bess with me.

My wife, Jan, was in hospital having had one of her many operations. An elderly friend who lives along the road offered to look after Bess whenever such occasions arose. She had an ageing German Shepherd Dog and both animals enjoyed each other's company.

One day my control room contacted me on the radio and asked me to get in touch with the lady. As soon as I could I went there. It appeared that Bess had had a bad turn and was fading fast. Her colitis was taking its toll despite a stringent diet and medication.

I took her straight to our vet, who, by his expertise and concern for a fine old dog, was able to rally her. I was dreading how I would tell Jan, in hospital, if anything should have happened to Bess.

116

That weekend Jan came home from hospital and was given a tremendous welcome by both Bess and Jo.

That very same night Bess's breathing became laboured and she was off colour again. I telephoned the vet at his home and he told me to keep her warm. I put her on a blanket in the doorway of our bedroom so that she would have company.

It took her a long time to settle and even after she went to sleep, I lay there just mulling over things that we had been through together.

I must have dozed off because at 2 o'clock I was startled by a deep sigh. I went to her and she was on her side. Her eyes were open but I am sure that they were unseeing. Her tongue lolled out.

As I crouched down beside her she raised her head slightly but it was such an effort. Her tail just about moved as she welcomed me to her.

I could see that she was going. I cradled her head in my lap. Another sigh and Bess was gone. I sat there for ages, wondering if she had rallied the first time just so that she could see Jan again.

Why do they not last longer? If only all police dogs could be as reliable as this old girl had been.

She looked out of the ordinary so therefore had a character all of her own. She was remembered by all who saw her at demonstrations and fêtes. She was admired by football fans, even those who had come to know the other side of her nature. She had worked her heart out for me and I could not have asked for more. She had saved my skin on more than one occasion.

To cap it all, only that day I had been discussing with Jan the fact that Jo was not coming up to standard as a police dog and would have to be replaced. Jo was such a lovely dog and we would have loved to keep her, but to have three German Shepherds around the place would not be practical. We certainly could not part with Bessie and we would have to have Jo's replacement at home. So, very reluctantly, we decided that Jo would have to be found a new home.

Bessie even sorted out that problem for us.

'Bye Bess.'

THE TRIALS SCHEDULE

PART 1 — GENERAL OBEDIENCE

TEST 1

a. **Heel Free**

The test will be carried out at the slow, normal or double pace, as the judge directs. The 'right', 'left' and 'about' turns are to be demonstrated at the command of the Judge. At each halt the dog will remain in the 'sit', 'stand' or 'down' position as the Judge directs.

b. **Sendaway and Re-direction**

The dog will be required, upon command of the handler, to go to a specified point indicated by the Judge. This distance will be not less than 40 yards or more than 150 yards. Upon direction of the Judge, the dog will be sent to another specified point, being a distance of not less than 40 yards or more than 100 yards.

c. **Retrieve**

The dog will retrieve any article (excluding those made of glass or with a sharp edge) which, in the opinion of the Judge, it is likely to encounter when operational. The dog must not move forward to 'retrieve' or 'deliver to hand on return' until commanded to do so by the handler on direction of the Judge.

d. **Agility**
i. **Obstacle Jump — Three Feet**

The dog should be sent forward to clear the obstacle upon command of the handler, without touching it with its feet or hindquarters, and upon further command, remain stationary. The handler will be directed to rejoin the dog to complete the exercise. The dog will be allowed one attempt only.

ii. **Scale — Six Feet**

Upon command of the handler, the dog will be sent forward to scramble the obstacle and on further command will remain stationary, in any position, at the other side. At the direction of the Judge the dog will be recalled over the obstacle to rejoin its handler. The normal 'sit' in front of the handler and the finish to heel will be included in this exercise. The dog will be allowed only one attempt in either direction.

iii. Long Jump — Nine Feet

The dog will be required by the handler to clear the obstacle without touching it with its feet or hindquarters and, upon further command, remain stationary in any position on command of the handler. The handler, upon direction of the Judge, will then rejoin his dog, thus completing the exercise.

e. 'Speak' on Command

The handler will command or signal his dog to bark under the direction of the Judge and it should do so quite firmly and continuously. The dog should immediately respond to command or signal from the handler and failure to do so, or any undue assistance, will be penalised.

f. 'Down' Handler Out of Sight

The dog will be required to remain in the 'down' position for the full period of 10 minutes, with the handler out of sight. The Judge may cause the temperament of the dog to be tested by sending persons to walk round it, or causing diversionary noises to be made.

PART 1 — CRIMINAL WORK

Chase and Attack

The 'criminal' will run away and on the direction of the Judge, the handler will order his dog to chase and attack. The attack will be done in a clean and determined manner, but without any undue excitement, viciousness or apprehension. The dog must satisfy the Judge that he is capable of preventing the escape of a determined 'criminal'. If the 'criminal' escapes, no marks will be awarded.

After the attack, the search and escort of the prisoner will be carried out.

Chase and Stand Off

The dog will be required to chase, on command, a running person. This person will leave his place of concealment and commence to run away, thus arousing the handler's suspicions. The handler will, on the direction of the Judge, order his dog to chase. The running man, as the dog approaches, will stop and face the dog, where upon the dog will circle and bark, and give clear indication that he is preventing the man's escape, until the arrival of the handler. All undue excitement, viciousness, apprehension or biting will be penalised. All additional commands will be penalised.

Test of Courage — Stick Attack

The dog will be required to engage a determined 'criminal' who is armed with a stick which is used to deter the attack. The dog will make a spontaneous and determined attack and any encouragement by the handler will be penalised.

Test of Courage — Gun
The dog will be required to resolutely attack a 'criminal' armed with a gun, regardless of gunfire and without undue viciousness or apprehension.

PART 2 — NOSEWORK, TRACKING AND SEARCHING

TEST 1

a. **Track**

Leash track, about half a mile long and approximately two hours old, to be laid by a person other than the handler. Four track-layer's articles will be dropped on the track. The handler will inform the Judge prior to the commencement of the track the method in which the dog will indicate the articles.

TEST 2

a. **Searching for Property**

The dog will be required to search for and find in a defined area, three articles bearing scent. The three articles are to be retrieved. The search area will not exceed 25 yards square and the handler, whilst free to exercise discretion as to his own positioning, must not enter the area. Five minutes will be allowed for this test.

b. **Indication of an Irretrievable Article**

The dog is required to search for and find an irretrievable article and indicate its presence by barking.

c. **Search for Hidden Person**

The dog will be required to search for 2 separate persons, both concealed; one in an accessible position and the other inaccessible. The hidden persons will be located in two distinctly different places within the search area.

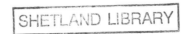

Meresborough Books

17 Station Road, Rainham, Gillingham, Kent. ME8 7RS
Telephone: Medway (0634) 388812

We are a specialist publisher of books about Kent. Our books are available in most bookshops in the county, including our own at this address. Alternatively you may order direct, adding 10% for post (minimum 50p, orders over £30 post free). ISBN prefix 0 905270 for 3 figure numbers, 094819 for 4 figure numbers. Titles in print December 1992.

HARDBACKS

AIRCRAFT CASUALTIES IN KENT Part One 1939-40 compiled by G.G. Baxter, K.A. Owen and P. Baldock. ISBN 3506. £12.95.

BARGEBUILDING ON THE SWALE by Don Sattin. ISBN 3530. £9.95.

EDWARDIAN CHISLEHURST by Arthur Battle. ISBN 3433. £9.95.

FISHERMEN FROM THE KENTISH SHORE by Derek Coombe. ISBN 3409. £10.95.

THE HISTORY OF THE ROYAL SEA BATHING HOSPITAL, MARGATE 1791-1991 by F.G. St Clair Strange. ISBN 3573. £12.95.

JUST OFF THE SWALE by Don Sattin. ISBN 045. £5.95.

KENT: A PORTRAIT IN COLOUR by John Guy. ISBN 3700. £12.95.

KENT'S OWN by Robin J. Brooks. The history of 500 (County of Kent) Squadron of the R.A.A.F. ISBN 541. £5.95.

THE LONDON, CHATHAM & DOVER RAILWAY by Adrian Gray. ISBN 886. £7.95.

A NEW DICTIONARY OF KENT DIALECT by Alan Major. ISBN 274. £7.50.

THE PAST GLORY OF MILTON CREEK by Alan Cordell and Leslie Williams. ISBN 3042. £9.95.

THE PLACE NAMES OF KENT by Judith Glover. ISBN 614. £7.50. BARGAIN OFFER £4.95.

ROCHESTER FROM OLD PHOTOGRAPHS compiled by the City of Rochester Society. Large format. ISBN 975. £7.95.(Also available in paperback ISBN 983. £4.95.)

SHERLOCK HOLMES AND THE KENT RAILWAYS by Kelvin Jones. ISBN 3255. £8.95.

A SIDEWAYS LAUNCH by Anne Salmon. ISBN 3689. £15.95.

STRATFORD HOUSE SCHOOL 1912-1987 by Susan Pittman. ISBN 3212. £10.00.

TALES OF VICTORIAN HEADCORN or The Oddities of Heddington by Penelope Rivers (Ellen M. Poole). ISBN 3050. £8.95. (Also available in paperback ISBN 3069. £3.95).

TEYNHAM MANOR AND HUNDRED (798-1935) by Elizabeth Selby, MBE. ISBN 630. £5.95.

TROOPSHIP TO CALAIS by Derek Spiers. ISBN 3395. £11.95.

TWO HALVES OF A LIFE by Doctor Kary Pole. ISBN 509. £5.95.

US BARGEMEN by A.S. Bennett. ISBN 207. £6.95.

A VIEW OF CHRIST'S COLLEGE, BLACKHEATH by A.E.O. Crombie, B.A. ISBN 223. £6.95.

LARGE FORMAT PICTORIAL PAPERBACKS

ARE YOU BEING SERVED, MADAM? by Molly Proctor. ISBN 3174. £3.50.

BEFORE AND AFTER THE HURRICANE IN AND AROUND CANTERBURY by Paul Crampton. ISBN 3387. £3.50. BARGAIN £1.95.

THE BLITZ OF CANTERBURY by Paul Crampton. ISBN 3441. £3.50.

CANTERBURY BEFORE THE BLITZ by Paul Crampton. ISBN 3662. £4.95.

CANTERBURY THEN AND NOW by Paul Crampton. ISBN 359X. £3.95.

CLIFFE IN OLD PHOTOGRAPHS by Allan Cherry. ISBN 362X. £3.95.

EAST KENT FROM THE AIR by John Guy. ISBN 3158. £3.50.
EAST SUSSEX RAILWAYS IN OLD POSTCARDS by Kevin Robertson. ISBN 3220.
£3.50.
GEORGE BARGEBRICK Esq. by Richard-Hugh Perks. ISBN 479. £4.50.
HEADCORN: A Pictorial History by the Headcorn Local History Society. ISBN
3271. £3.50.
KENT TOWN CRAFTS by Richard Filmer. ISBN 584. £2.95.
LENHAM AND BOUGHTON MALHERBE IN OLD PHOTOGRAPHS by Jean
Cockett and Amy Myers. ISBN 3646. £3.95.
THE LIFE AND ART OF ONE MAN by Dudley Pout. ISBN 525. £2.95.
THE MEDWAY TOWNS FROM THE AIR by Piers Morgan and Diane Nicholls. ISBN
3557. £4.95.
MORE PICTURES OF RAINHAM by Barbara Mackay Miller. ISBN 3298. £3.50.
THE MOTOR BUS SERVICES OF KENT AND EAST SUSSEX — A brief history by Eric
Baldock. ISBN 959. £4.95.
OLD BROADSTAIRS by Michael David Mirams. ISBN 3115. £3.50.
OLD CHATHAM: A THIRD PICTURE BOOK by Philip MacDougall. ISBN 3190.
£3.50. BARGAIN £1.95.
OLD FAVERSHAM by Arthur Percival. ISBN 3425. £3.50.
OLD GILLINGHAM by Philip MacDougall. ISBN 3328. £3.50.
OLD MAIDSTONE Vol.3 by Irene Hales. ISBN 3336. £3.50. BARGAIN £1.95.
OLD MARGATE by Michael David Mirams. ISBN 851. £3.50.
OLD PUBS OF TUNBRIDGE WELLS & DISTRICT by Keith Hetherington and Alun
Griffiths. ISBN 300X. £3.50.
OLD RAMSGATE by Michael David Mirams. ISBN 797. £3.50.
PEMBURY IN THE PAST by Mary Standen. ISBN 916. £2.95.
A PICTORIAL HISTORY OF COOLING AND CLIFFE by Allan Cherry. ISBN 376X.
£3.95.
A PICTORIAL STUDY OF ALKHAM PARISH by Susan Lees and Roy Humphreys.
ISBN 3034. £2.95.
A PICTORIAL STUDY OF HAWKINGE PARISH by Roy Humphreys. ISBN 328X.
£3.50.
A PICTUREBOOK OF OLD NORTHIAM by Lis Rigby. ISBN 3492. £3.95.
A PICTUREBOOK OF OLD RAINHAM by Barbara Mackay Miller. ISBN 606. £3.50.
REMINISCENCES OF OLD CRANBROOK by Joe Woodcock. ISBN 331X. £3.50.
ROCHESTER FROM OLD PHOTOGRAPHS — see under hardbacks.
SMARDEN: A Pictorial History by Jenni Rodger. ISBN 592. £3.50.
STEAM SCENE AT TONBRIDGE by Mike Feaver. ISBN 3670. £3.95.
THOMAS SIDNEY COOPER OF CANTERBURY by Brian Stewart. ISBN 762. £2.95.
TRANSPORT IN KENT 1900-1938 by Eric Baldock. ISBN 3603. £3.95.
WEST KENT FROM THE AIR by John Guy. ISBN 3166. £3.50.

STANDARD SIZE PAPERBACKS

BIRDS OF KENT: A Review of their Status and Distribution by the Kent Ornitho-
logical Society. ISBN 800. £6.95.
BIRDWATCHING IN KENT by Don Taylor. ISBN 932. £4.50.
THE CANTERBURY MONSTERS by John H. Vaux. ISBN 3468. £2.50.
THE CHATHAM DOCKYARD STORY by Philip MacDougall. ISBN 3301. £6.95.
CHIDDINGSTONE — AN HISTORICAL EXPLORATION by Jill Newton. ISBN 940.
£1.95.
A CHRONOLOGY OF ROCHESTER by Brenda Purle. ISBN 851. £1.50.
THE CHURCH AND VILLAGE OF TUNSTALL by Arthur A. Midwinter. ISBN 3697.
£3.95.
COBHAM. Published for Cobham Parish Council. ISBN 3123. £1.00.
CRIME AND CRIMINALS IN VICTORIAN KENT by Adrian Gray. ISBN 967. £3.95.

CYCLE TOURS OF KENT by John Guy. No. 1: Medway, Gravesend, Sittingbourne and Sheppey. ISBN 517. £1.50.
EXPLORING KENT CHURCHES by John E. Vigar. ISBN 3018. £3.95.
EXPLORING SUSSEX CHURCHES by John E. Vigar. ISBN 3093. £3.95.
FLIGHT IN KENT. ISBN 3085. £1.95.
FROM MOTHS TO MERLINS: The History of West Malling Airfield by Robin J. Brooks. ISBN 3239. £4.95.
THE GHOSTS OF KENT by Peter Underwood. ISBN 86X. £3.95.
HAWKINGE 1912-1961 by Roy Humphreys. ISBN 3522. £8.95.
A HISTORY OF CHATHAM GRAMMAR SCHOOL FOR GIRLS, 1907-1982 by Audrey Perkyns. ISBN 576. £1.95.
THE HOP BIN by Geoff & Fran Doel. ISBN 3735. £5.95.
IN BAGGY BROWN BREECHES by Norah Turner. ISBN 3654. £4.95.
KENT AIRFIELDS IN THE BATTLE OF BRITAIN by the Kent Aviation Historical Research Society. ISBN 3247. £5.95.
KENT AND EAST SUSSEX UNDERGROUND by The Kent Underground Research Group. ISBN 3581. £5.95.
KENT COUNTRY CHURCHES by James Antony Syms. ISBN 3131. £4.50.
KENT COUNTRY CHURCHES CONTINUED by James Antony Syms. ISBN 314X. £5.95.
KENT COUNTRY CHURCHES CONCLUDED by James Antony Syms. ISBN 345X. £5.95.
KENT INNS AND SIGNS by Michael David Mirams. ISBN 3182. BARGAIN £2.50.
LET'S EXPLORE THE RIVER DARENT by Frederick Wood. ISBN 770. £1.95.
LETTER TO MARSHY by Barbara Trigg. ISBN 3727. £3.95.
LULLINGSTONE PARK: THE EVOLUTION OF A MEDIAEVAL DEER PARK by Susan Pittman. ISBN 703. £3.95.
MARDEN: A WEALDEN VILLAGE by Phyllis Highwood and Peggy Skelton. ISBN 3107. £4.95.
MUMMING, HOWLING AND HOODENING by Geoff & Fran Doel. ISBN 3743. £3.50.
OFF THE BEATEN TRACK by Geoffrey Hufton. ISBN 3751. £3.50.
ONE DOG AND HER MAN by Ted Wright. ISBN 3719. £5.95.
PENINSULA ROUND (The Hoo Peninsula) by Des Worsdale. ISBN 568. £1.50.
PRELUDE TO WAR: Aviation in Kent 1938-39 by KAHRS. ISBN 3476. £2.50.
RADIO KENT GARDENERS' GUIDE by Harry Smith and Bob Collard. ISBN 3549. £3.95.
SAINT ANDREW'S CHURCH, DEAL by Gregory Holyoake. ISBN 835. 95p.
THE SCHOOL ON THE BALL FIELDS (CRANBROOK) by Mary Standen. ISBN 3638. £5.95.
SHORNE: The History of a Kentish Village by A.F. Allen. ISBN 3204. £4.95.
SIR GARRARD TYRWHITT-DRAKE AND THE COBTREE ESTATE, MAIDSTONE by Elizabeth Melling B.A. ISBN 3344. £1.50.
SITTINGBOURNE & KEMSLEY LIGHT RAILWAY STOCKBOOK AND GUIDE. ISBN 843. 95p.
STEAM IN MY FAMILY by John Newton. ISBN 3417. £4.95.
STOUR VALLEY WALKS from Canterbury to Sandwich by Christopher Donaldson. ISBN 991. £1.95.
TALES OF VICTORIAN HEADCORN — see under hardbacks.
TARGET FOLKESTONE by Roy Humphreys. ISBN 3514. £7.95.
WADHURST: Town of the High Weald by Alan Savidge and Oliver Mason. ISBN 3352. £5.95.
WARTIME KENT 1939-40 compiled by Oonagh Hyndman from the BBC Radio Kent broadcasts. ISBN 3611. £6.95.
WHERE NO FLOWERS GROW by George Glazebrook. ISBN 3379. £2.50.
WHO'S BURIED WHERE IN KENT by Alan Major. ISBN 3484. £5.95.